A Master's in Love &
a Bachelor's in Growth

A Master's in Love &
a Bachelor's in Growth

Carl M. Watson

Rev. date: 10/03/2019

To order additional copies of this book, contact:
Xlibris
1-888-795-4274
www.Xlibris.com
Orders@Xlibris.com
761799

Welcome to the Undergrad Level -

Our Bachelor's in Growth Journey

LEARNING OBJECTIVES IN GROWTH

LEARNING OBJECTIVES IN LOVE

Growth Syllabus

T HE PURPOSE OF this page is to shed some light on the journey you are about to undergo. The undergrad journey does vastly differ from the graduate journey. Though it may only be the bachelor's degree section, this section is vital in order to succeed in the areas of love and relationship. However, this is not set up like your average university system. If you have arrived here for love stories, situationships, romance, or simply moments that you deal with when interacting and dating, feel free to skip ahead. Be sure you know how to love yourself first.

Yet before you do so, allow me to reveal a little about this section. This section is not necessarily here to lecture you as much as it is to show and reiterate the greatness and potential within you. It is here to encourage and support your progress and growth process. This section is proof that someone believes in your potential to be great as long as you have a desire to improve. Lastly, it is here to say "yes, you can."

I ask that as you go through each different piece and allow them to resonate with you by finding how they relate to moments in your life—past, present, or future. Whether they are memories or events you foresee occurring or have occurred, write them down. These may all be things you've learned about yourself or encountered, but so have I. So let's turn this into our journey.

If no one else told you today, I'm proud of any decision you have made to better yourself and become great! So be great because you have every right to greatness. Then stay great because progress only stops when time does. This goes for progress in all areas of your life: family life, financial life, spiritual life, etc. With that being said, welcome!

Fear's Hunger

IT'S AN OVERWHELMING feeling with a beastly appetite,
Devouring every inch of confidence.
Anxiety fuels its adrenaline.
Fear is swiftly consuming hope, and feasting on all doubt
Triggering a time freeze.
The thoughts in your mind wander as if in a tunnel –
A tunnel whose darkness is so loud
That you begin to see things in the dark.
Will it end?
Will there even be a light at the end of the tunnel,
Or is the path an endless cave?
Pumping, pulsating, and with blood racing—
The heart aggressively pries its way out.
Puncturing through the chest, it prepares to jump,
Just to evade fear.
Consequently and simultaneously,
The brain's speed decreases exponentially.
Then the power shuts down.
And words begin to . . .
Words begin to . . .
Error, error.
"Error 6923 has occurred."
Suddenly, it's over.

Fear is fed.

The power returns followed by spontaneous lights.

The heart fixes his home and repairs the damage.

Like a town in Tornado Alley,

Everything returns to normal as if nothing happened

While they wait for the next beastly attack.

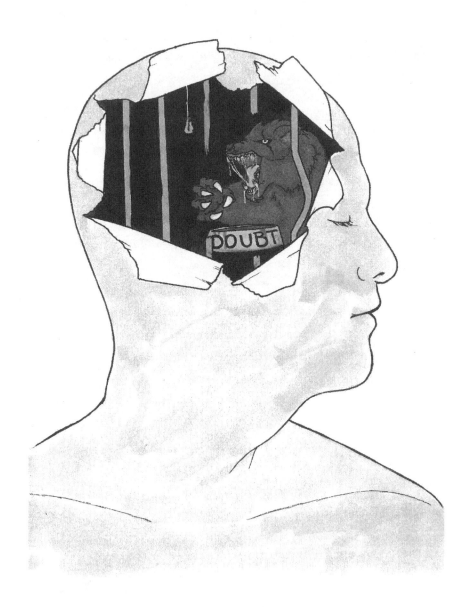

What's Up? Talk to Me!   Fear's Hunger

Make no mistake, fear can be a serious adversary with lethal consequences in some cases. So acknowledge the harmful fear and then take the necessary action to clobber and conquer it.

Is/are fear(s) holding captive something you want or need? If so, what fear(s) is/are standing in your way right now?

_____

What's a fear you've overcome that was a major milestone in your life?

_____

How did you do it?

_____

_____

_____

www.thecmwexperience.com

Check out the blog section of the book's website for the full experience.

Night Thoughts

ALONE WITH MY thoughts or rather
Alone with the endless whys, hows, whens, and which ones.
I twist and turn while reflecting on the happenings in my life.
Memories of never fully playing ball for the school team,
Never truly having time for an official girlfriend,
And times when I was struck by fear
Are all sent into my limbic and cortex.
In search of how to improve to reach satisfaction,
I realize satisfaction is only a limitation
That I want to exceed, so I strive for perfection.
Sometimes an unattainable goal . . .
With that in mind, I set a daily aspiration known as
Carpe diem – to seize the day.
Maximize the moment.
Capture what's present – don't let it slip away.
Then there is this insufferable thought of loneliness or
Rather a black hole that continually tries to steal my joy . . . .
But this black hole never seems to leave home without his friend failure.
Sometimes failure's brother fear pays a visit.
Failure and fear – together they work fiercely to obstruct one's
Destination or skew one's view.
I have faced failure and I've been surrounded by fear,
But my attitude . . . I cannot lose!

I have no regrets . . . that which has occurred has occurred for a reason.

The boogeyman that hides under my bed

Is manifested by not living up to expectations.

The fact of the matter is that fear and failing are

Intertwined, interrelated, twisted, and braided.

The fear of not achieving greatness!

The fear of not being the hero everyone is counting on me to become!

The fear of not making everyone who has invested so much in me . . .

Proud.

Luckily, there is a thought that banishes the boogeyman

And calms the storm...

Or rather my faith, and memories of triumph

Assure me that no matter what,

God will never leave nor forsake me!

Through Him, I can do all things!

He is my confidence!

He will perfect that which concerns me!

I can always go to sleep knowing God will always make a way . . .

Night thoughts that turn into morning joy!

What's Up? Talk to Me! Night Thoughts

"Most great people have attained their success just one step beyond their greatest failure." Napoleon Hill

Do you ever take time to reflect on your life?

_____

Are you left encouraged or discouraged after reflecting?

_____

What do you see after revisiting your failures and accomplishments?

_____

What triumphs do you remember?

_____

_____

_____

www.thecmwexperience.com

Check out the blog section of the book's website for the full experience.

Image of Greatness

S TOP, YOU . . . wait!
Stop! Who? You!
No one has the God-given ability to stop you
. . . To stop your greatness!
Except, well . . . you, but you've heard this all before.
Allow me to help you look through these binoculars,
So you can see your future clearer.
Where, in any verse in the Bible or books of higher power does it say
You were placed here with the purpose to perish or fail?
An omnipotent and limitless God has made you in His image.
Even with your human flaws,
Your essence alone equates to nothing less than great.
If this is true,
Then why do some not reach their full potential or succeed in life?
This is a question that correlates to many problems and answers.

The size of your obstacle?
You may allow a pothole to turn into a pitfall!
Negativity only breeds negativity,
Creating a snowball effect of unwanted
Thoughts, feelings, and energy.
At times, this leads to the manifestation of negative events
Or even negative people.

It is almost like your mind has become a magnet

That strengthens in negativity the more you feed it negativity.

Wait! Is it really that bad?

Crossbreed with some positivity. Find the bright side, and find a solution.

Withdraw joyful moments of your life from your memory bank,

In abundance.

Allow your mind to feed off that,

Then see your obstacle for what it really is!

Not a mountain, but a molehill.

Sometimes this is easier said than done, but now it's your own

Personal, emotional, spiritual, or mental weakness that's trying to

Stop you.

Yet, you and I both know that these things can't really stop you

Because they are easily reinforced with faith and optimism.

You're not alone.

This is where your faith in God or your higher power becomes

Your lifeline.

Zoom in – adjust ever so slightly – can you see that great person yet?

Some support?

You may just need someone to say, "You can and will do it."

Someone to say, "I believe in you."

Wait, have you not been paying attention?

I do. I believe in you!

If you are striving to progress and improve, then I am proud of you.

Surround yourself with like-minded people,

Who want to see you in the winner's circle with them.

Don't be oblivious.

The fact is you have fans in the stands where there are cheers

Just for you.

Regardless how small or big

Whispers or roars,

Head nods or body waves,

Snaps or handclaps.

There is someone there.

Do you see that unstoppable, unbothered, unmovable

Force of nature when you look in the mirror?

Overanalyzing?

Are you overthinking?

They say too much of anything can be bad for you.

What is happening here is you create a "what if" cell or

An "I don't know if" cell in your mind.

These cells are fine, until you begin to dwell on them.

Over and over again, you magnify their growth.

Now instead of following its normal cellular process of growing,

By dividing into other ideas, and fading away, it just grows.

It grows uncontrollably and morphs into a cancer

That attacks your mind and heart.

Slowly killing feelings of audacity and ambition.

Killing thoughts of success and accomplishment. So

let that cell run its course and die.

If overanalyzing has become an issue,

Allow your actions to solve the problem.

Sometimes doing so trumps thinking.

Take a leap of faith.

If you don't fly the first time, maybe you'll learn to

Swim when you hit the water.

Now has the blurred focus become clearer? Can you see?

Can you now see that person bearing immense amounts of

Greatness right in front of you?

Can you finally see you?

What are some major obstacles in your life that have become a lot smaller once you have faced them?

_____

Compose a small list of people that believe in you (yes, there is at least one). They can be coworkers, pets, preachers, teachers, loved ones that may have passed, etc. All count.

_____

Do you overthink at times, especially about something you really care about?

_____

Well, hey cut that out!

_____

_____

_____

www.thecmwexperience.com

Check out the blog section of the book's website for the full experience.

Ask Yourself

F OR WHAT?
It doesn't make you happy.
For what?

It's not fun.

For what?

It's not fulfilling!

. . . Why do you do it?

"Because!"

"It makes me money,"

"Right?"

"Because!"

"It's work and everyone has to,"

"Right?"

"Because!"

"It fills me with pride"

"I know that one is right."

". . . Right?"

Okay,

You chose this (**J**)ustification for your (**O**)bligation to this (**B**)usiness

. . . Your J.O.B

If you had the choice, would you stay here?

Here in your current state?

Here in your current job position?

The position in which most of your current life decisions orbit around.

. . . No?

No.

But you do have the choice!

Maybe it's not the life you have chosen,

But you choose how you live it!

. . . So what will you do?

"I don't know."

And that's okay. It's normal.

Just ask yourself,

What will bring you bliss? Now ask yourself,

What steps should you take?

Ask yourself, because only you truly know the answer.

What's Up? Talk to Me!   Ask Yourself

Are you happy with where you are in life, job-wise or in general?

_____

What situation or circumstance is hindering you? What's keeping you from where you want to be?

_____

What is your plan of action to change things (even if the actions are minor)?

_____

_____

_____

www.thecmwexperience.com

Check out the blog section of the book's website for the full experience.

The Nest (Fall or Flight)

I
T'S SO HIGH!
The mere sight of the ground
Pumps your stomach with butterflies and anxiety.
This alone makes the nest feel that much more comfortable, a.k.a. safer.
Yet, the height of the nest is superseded by the view of the limitless sky.
The very fiber of your being yearns to take flight and leave the nest.
The sight of the blue sky fuels your excitement, ambition, and joy.
You know you are born to fly. It's as simple as animal instincts.
Wait, but there are thoughts and questions that attack your mind
Like an angry swarm of bees.
When is the right time?
Do I know enough to fly?
What if I hit the ground?
What if it rains when I try?
What if something else knocks me out of the sky?
. . . But what if you fly?
Every small goal accomplished,
Every small action taken is a step closer to the edge of the nest.
With every step, your foot firmly plants into the oh-so-familiar nest.
Suppressing it beneath your feet, making a stand to surly depart,
Only to remain.
However, you know that you are now that much closer.
The fall . . . no I mean – the ground full of

Doubt, disappointment, and pain.

The ground, full of lessons, drive, and motivation.

As always, your heart, your mind, and your soul meet

On the stage of life for another battle.

Do you take the leap?

Did you take the leap?

Will you take the leap?

Your purpose in life does not revolve around the nest or the ground.

It lies in the sky. It's tied to the sky.

If you are unsure,

Just know there was a reason you were born with wings.

Your sky awaits.

No, your future awaits. I'm waiting on you,

But how long will you wait?

What's Up? Talk to Me! The Nest (Fall or Flight)

What's a goal or dream that your doubt has you too paralyzed to at least try (big or small)? Maybe things like job positions, leadership roles, crushes, working out, or writing a book.

_____

Why do you think you can't?

_____

Now how can you?

_____

_____

_____

www.thecmwexperience.com

Check out the blog section of the book's website for the full experience.

You Versus . . .

F**K.

How do you describe the feeling . . .
Or the lack thereof?

Imagine you stand tall at five foot even,

And before you stands a seven- foot-one figure.

A figure you seemed to have gotten along with in the past.

In fact, there were times you felt as though you two

Could have been friends.

But like fungus, an unexpected tension begins to fester.

Over the course of time,

The actions of this figure became more and more hostile.

As if the only way to remove this fungus was to remove you.

Now here you two stand.

Your forehead begins to emit a shine, and your pores are now opening.

The sun is scorching everything it touches.

Even through your shoes, it feels like the pavement is on fire,

But you're wrong.

It's not the sun you feel . . .

It's the heat from the tension between you two.

The fire in your big bold eyes burn with blue flames . . .

But this figure's eyes have a blaze like no other,

As if you're staring at the surface of the sun.

For a split second, you wonder how it came to this.

. . . *Bam!*. . . *"What the heck!"*

All thoughts are lost along with your balance.

A fist and your face collided at the speed of sound.

After finding your balance, adrenaline shoves the feeling of pain away

As you lunge forward at the figure

With the reach of a giant, the strength of an ape, and fists like concrete,

You are struck again by the figure!

This time your hands and the pavement meet abruptly,

And shortly you rise again.

And again, you are reintroduced to the ground.

Again, you try, and again you become one with the pavement.

Then again and again until the ground becomes more and more

Comfortable.

The thought of quitting becomes more and more pleasant.

The idea slowly seeps deeper and deeper into your mind,

Like an IV into your vein.

The flames in your eyes begin to fade until they are replaced

With a cold, hollow darkness.

Even pain walked away accompanied by anger and sadness.

Why fight it? Stay down, and the whole ordeal will be over . . . right?

Right!

But there is *so* much better in store for you.

Your dreams, your joy, your love . . . your victory is all contingent upon

The strength of your legs to stand again.

And so you do just that. You stand.

You stand beaten, battered, and bruised.

You stand tall at six feet five inches because

Now you stand with your God-given ability to overcome!

Now you notice a new figure behind you, so much bigger than

The both of you that it looked like the sky had opened.

As you stare this figure called, Life, into its eyes, the figure behind you

Says something:

"Move by faith, not by sight."

What happens next?

Well, you're David, and life is Goliath . . .

What's Up? Talk to Me!   You Versus . . .

What's the most recent major issue or problem life has hit you with?

_____

Did you already overcome and get back up?

_____

If so, I want to say, "I've been telling you that you could, champ!"

_____

If not, do you know that you can? I'm serious! You really can, which is what I need to convey to you, champ!

_____

_____

_____

www.thecmwexperience.com

Check out the blog section of the book's website for the full experience.

From Boss to Boss

MAYBE YOU HAVE forgotten who and what you are . . . or Maybe you just need a reminder.

I am here to relay the message from your inner boss.

What's up, boss?

Yeah, you, the one that conquers regardless of the cost,

Regardless of the loss.

Constantly cooking up a recipe for success

With your own special source.

You know, your special flare and flavor.

Those characteristics combined to compose your winning charisma.

Charisma your fans want to savor,

Or maybe it's your haters.

There's an aura around your life.

Some would call it favor.

So you're saying your power comes from above?

So you're supported by a power that won't nudge?

But hey, who am I to judge?

I mean, I'm only you, and I've been spectating.

But sometimes, it's devastating

When you forget that you are great.

Now give birth to something magnificent.

Let's see the fruits of your labor.

We're all waiting on the due date,

Gathered around your campfire with tents.

So many voting for you to win. You must be running for mayor.

This is your scene, and you're the director.

So kill the doubt and the fear off because they're just extras

Being extra and dramatic,

And trying wreak havoc.

Now you must take your place on the throne

Because they won't just let you have it.

What's Up? Talk to Me!   From Boss to Boss

Check this out. Did you know that you were a winner? Have you always known this about yourself?

_____

If not, do you now know inside that there is a winner? There is a right answer to that question, and I am sure you know it.

_____

_____

_____

www.thecmwexperience.com

Check out the blog section of the book's website for the full experience.

The Family You Chose

MANY SAY YOU can't pick your family.
. . . I guess that's true?

These annoying people who seem to

Have a schematic to Your emotions

Because they always know what buttons to press.

These people, who you are always trying to please or impress.

These people you hold on to,

Like a life vest when your boat is being rocked

Because you trust in the security they provide when hit with those tides.

They are a double-edged sword.

They are there to defend you even when you are wrong

And there to tell you, "You know better," or "you're doing wrong."

Sometimes the feeling is like a quick pinch

When these people hit you with an "I told you," or "I knew it."

These individuals are the ones you are proud to see succeed,

As if your support was the boost that helped propel them forward.

At times, these people are so important,

They play the roles of your panel of judges

As you confide in them for ratings on your life decisions.

At times, these people are important enough to play board of directors

As you search for approval.

These are the geniuses that cause you to say things like

"How did I get into this?" "Smart move," "I can't stand you,"

"Why would you do that?" and "What in the world…?
All said out of joy, anger, and laughter.
These are the beings that take and borrow everything
From food to clothes,
Leaving you with a return process that gets more convoluted than
Affairs at a financial-aid office.
These people believe in your potential and in your dreams.
They may make fun of you, but they would always respect you for
Who you are and who you can be.
They are the people, who have your back while standing
In front of you waiting for something to pop off.
With these people, time away changes nothing between you,
But time with them changes everything.
These are the beings you create moments and memories with.
These are the people you never have to say "I love you" to
Because it has always been implied.
But every now and then, you still might.
These people are known as your friends,
But they are described as your family.
These are the people you choose to be your friends.
These are the people you choose to be your family.
And if these things are true about the family you chose,
Then you made a great choice in friends.
So I guess the saying was erroneous,
You can choose your family!

What's Up? Talk to Me!   The Family You Chose

List a few of your closest friends that are like family.

_____

For each person, list something about them that demonstrates to you they are like family.

_____

_____

_____

www.thecmwexperience.com

Check out the blog section of the book's website for the full experience.

The Pressure

P RESSURE!
Pressure bursts pipes! Pressure makes diamonds!
Pressure is heavy . . . it's tight.
It squeezes you . . . tightly compressing, erasing, and eradicating
The space around you.

Pressure attempts to take.
It does this by forcing itself upon you.
It doesn't ask, it just does.
It does this by suffocating that which gives you life.
Whether it's things such as air, confidence, hope, joy, and faith.

Yet, this coin has two faces.

Pressure can squeeze and produce juice.
Pressure can push and produce life.
Pressure is sometimes a process that involves the removal
Of an ugly or undesired exterior.
Crumbs of fear fall – rolling down your shoulder.
With it, the dirt and dust of doubt – flees from your pants legs.
With this outer coating eliminated,
Your glow—no—your shine can begin to illuminate through.

. . . But

What if this pressure you are experiencing is self-inflicted?

What happens when expectations for yourself grab ahold

And slowly apply pressure?

Its strength grows.

Its weight grows.

Yet, you seem to shrink

You embrace it!

But you do so in moderation.

Let that pressure and expectation be your fuel.

But don't crush yourself to achieve your dreams and goals,

Release some of the pressure and tension.

Try carrying the weight of the world one continent at a time.

What's Up? Talk to Me!   The Pressure

Do you put pressure on yourself because you have high expectations for yourself and because of the expectations of those around you?

_____

What is expected of you that is causing you pressure?

_____

Can you meet or exceed those expectations?

_____

There is a right answer. If you couldn't, why would it be expected of you? Unless it was something you never really wanted in the first place.

_____

_____

_____

www.thecmwexperience.com

Check out the blog section of the book's website for the full experience.

A Meeting

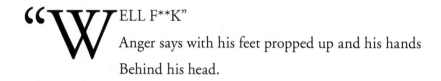

"**W**ELL F**K"
Anger says with his feet propped up and his hands
Behind his head.

"Now what?" He hits Hope with a condescending glare.
Hope has become hopeless which is very rare.
Then rocketing up out of his seat, stood Fear.
Frantically, he yells, "Clearly, Hope doesn't have the answers."
Fear's negative words eat away at Joy like a rapid spreading poison.
Joy, like a set off bomb, begins to tick.
Suddenly, a new feeling enters the room and takes control of all of it.
It was a feeling of acceptance.
Anger is surprisingly calm.
Joy is no longer a ticking time bomb. Fear is now reserved and indifferent,
But there is an empty seat with someone missing.
Now all that lies there is a nameplate – A nameplate that spells Hope.

A projector displays a problematic, preposterous, incredibly
Increasing, frustrating failure against the wall.
They are aimlessly engulfed in photos and evidence of previous
Mistakes and failures
As time seems to stall.
Boom!
Free from its hinges, the front door falls.

Three figures appear, identities unclear.

Out of the shadows, the first figure is revealed.

Hope is back and accompanied by Faith and Will.

Weakened and bruised, yet together they look stronger than ever.

Joy, Fear, and Anger are surprised and confused, however

A more hopeful atmosphere creates ventilation.

Hope, Will, and Faith begin presenting their plan to move forward.

All while Joy, Fear, and Anger are still in awe and curious about their

Previous location.

Faith and Will were imprisoned in the heart,

Locked away in their own residence due to recent situations.

The recent failures had become viruses causing the brain system

Much devastation.

As a result, they were locked in the heart until Hope arrived.

The infected system created numerous rigorous obstacles of doubt.

However, with Faith, Hope, and Will, Doubt's mere existence is almost

Negated.

Now finally, the answer Anger has awaited.

Hope: *"We will firmly move forward with God by faith, not by sight."*

What's Up? Talk to Me! A Meeting

Can you name a few moments in your life where you made power decisions based on the possibilities of what could happen in the future and did not base them on the problems around you?

_____

_____

_____

Thank you.

www.thecmwexperience.com

Check out the blog section of the book's website for the full experience.

The Drive

WHAT IS THIS feeling of defeat?
Blinded by goals unmet
And hurt by desires unfulfilled.

It's like hail smashing against your windshield.

You're driving, yet at the moment your vision is impaired.

So even with so much drive, it's hard to steer.

You want to keep going because you know the final destination is near.

But without vision, off the path you could begin to veer.

But without vision, it's what we've all feared.

Without vision, there is no drive.

So you park . . .

You're parked, feeling stagnant.

So you're parked, hearing static.

The radio bears no good news.

So what's ahead is still unknown.

You now must choose!

You may return home

. . . If you wish.

But then what was the freaking point of all of this?

Or . . . you could remain in park

. . . Doing nothing

Just waiting

. . . For what?

You're swelled up with "ifs" and "buts"

. . . Doubts and distractions.

There is only one way to move forward.

. . . And that is to move strategic, steady and steadfast with all resilience

Forward!

Your car may even have passengers waiting and depending on you.

Regardless!

The choice is simple really and no longer yours. You have to *drive* !

What's Up? Talk to Me!   The Drive

What kind of car do you drive?

_____

What kind of car do you want to drive? Let your imagination carry you away.

_____

Thanks, I was just asking.

_____

Seriously, can you imagine you are in that car and it's fueled by your will and desire?

_____

Now do you see yourself pulling off toward your dreams and goals? If so, keep driving toward them.

_____

If not, make some changes, and get back on your road to success.

_____

_____

_____

www.thecmwexperience.com

Check out the blog section of the book's website for the full experience.

The Hands That Helped

HANDS DESTROY AND hands build;
Hands kill and hands give life;
Hands help and hands hinder;
Hands shun and hands embrace;
Hands have the capacity to uplift and to let go.
What do you do with yours?

Held captive in your palms, in all our palms, is a power of
Such magnitude it can only be described as a God-given birthright.
The ability to make a difference, and the power to make an impact.
Unfortunately, hands can only reach so far, which is why we need vision.
Our sight is vital.
Why?
Well, are you able to see past yourself and into the world around you?
Those closest to you and the strangers around—can you see their
Struggles, their pitfalls, or their slight stumbles?
Maybe your vision stretches even farther.
Can your vision interpret problems in other countries, races, and places
Where a solution can't be found no matter how big or small?
While every problem you see is *not* your problem,
We must be aware that the world's problems are bigger than us.
If you are fully aware of a problem and you do nothing,
Does that make you a part of the problem or the solution?

Now that you have that sight, you can see where to place your hands.

Those hands can take many forms:

A hand of finance; a hand of compassion; a hand of consideration;

A physical hand of assistance; an uplifting hand; a hand of food,

Or be a helping hand with a smile, a joke, an "I'm proud of you,"

And an "I'm here if you need me."

These and many more are powers that lie dormant inside of you.

Keep in mind, you don't always have to go out of your way to help.

Nor do your gestures have to be monumental.

Yet when you do,

Remember that even a mustard seed grows because of nutrients.

So the next time help is requested,

Will you use those powerful hands to reject or to extend?

What's Up? Talk to Me!   The Hands That Helped

Who have you sincerely helped or blessed without any ulterior motives or personal benefits within the last week or last few days?

_____

What did you do?

_____

Why did you do it?

_____

What was their reaction?

_____

Thanks for doing that! It may seem like it could have gone unnoticed, but someone is always watching.

_____

_____

_____

www.thecmwexperience.com

Check out the blog section of the book's website for the full experience.

Almost

S HORT, AGAIN.
Not enough,
Again.
The finish line lies ahead with intoxicating temptation.
Your burning desire becomes fuel for each step.
. . . But
You lose traction with the turf, and a fight between your balance
And gravity breaks out.
You become the casualty of the fight as your face becomes one
With the turf.
. . . Inches from the finish line. Again!
But this time. . .
You've waited patiently for your turn in line.
Now your money sits in your wallet, anticipating its moment to shine.
The same money you spent 89.9 percent of your life
Trying to make on a daily basis.
With all you desire on the counter being rung up,
Soon needs and desires are fulfilled.
The cashier displays the price on the screen.
With excitement to fulfill those needs and desires,
You pull your money out to match their value.
Just to discover you didn't have enough money.

So . . . the time and work you invested to make the money was
Not enough to match the value of those needs and desires.

Again,
So close, just to fall short.
Never feeling tall enough for your favorite roller coaster
That you've always wanted to ride.

Again,
Yet . . .
These are not your generic random events. These are feelings . . .
This is how it feels to work for that goal, that dream, or that passion.
Only to be given an A for . . . Almost.
Yet!
This is no excuse to quit!
No excuse to accept anything less than the great things you desire;
The great things you deserve!
Only reasons.
Reasons to be given an
A for Always
A for Accomplish
A for Accurate
A for Astonishing
A for Advance
A for Astronomical
. . . An A for Another chance.

What's Up? Talk to Me!   Almost

What was your most current "almost" moment?

_____

Did you accomplish it?

_____

If so, keep it pushing superstar. Turn the page.

_____

If not, can you remember when you first started on this journey? Can you see how far you've come since then, dealing with whatever you had to deal with?

_____

Go make it happen!

_____

_____

_____

www.thecmwexperience.com

Check out the blog section of the book's website for the full experience.

Who Do You Work For?

*B*OOM! BONG!
Another excruciating collision. A fist-to-face crash on the highway to truth.

Splatter. The blood from your mouth paints the floor. Your left eye has a bruise that's replacing your eyebrow. Its size would lead some to believe it had its own gravitational pull—which would make sense, being that it keeps attracting fist after fist. Consequently, you still maintain an impaired sight. Your right one is slightly impaired as well, being that blood and sweat has found a home in this eye. Surprisingly, you are still able to make out a familiar face in front of you.

It's baffling . . . who do you know that could do this to you? Who do you know that can overpower you this way? Who do you know that's close enough to put you in a predicament such as this? Who do you know that would know just what to do and know just what to say to get you into this state you're currently in?

Boom!

The assailant: So! Who do you work for?

Even their voice sounds vaguely familiar over the ringing in your ears.

The assailant: You're making me do this! You are literally forcing my hand!

As he lifts you up by the collar, the chair rises with you. The chair is latched on to your wrist and legs as the rope digs into your skin.

The assailant: Is it Mike?

You ask yourself, "Who is Mike?," then words begin to form.

You: The guy from finance!

You respond with such a confused look on your bruised face.

He throws you to the ground, and you lie there on your scratched-up left arm.

The assailant: Funny guy, huh? Who do you work for?

Pow!

You: F**k!

You find a size ten and a half in your rib.

You think to yourself, *Mike's a close friend, but what would he have to do with this?*

The assailant: It is Pat!

You: *The one that's two cubicles down. We work together all the time and even hung out a couple of times . . . but why her?*

You: No, I don't know her that well!

Boom! A flawless shot to the face.

The assailant: Then it must be Betty!

You: *Well, yeah, she's on the board of directors, and we've had a long-standing relationship before that. Yet, I still don't know what she. . . .*

You: No! It's not!

He swiftly snatches you up, sitting your body up straight. Then he disappears into the shadows.

Sitting there with a single light beaming down over you, your breath begins to steady. The ringing in your ears is silenced, and your vision starts to return.

The assailant: It doesn't really matter who you work for . . . the problem is you were supposed to be working for me and our dreams!

Out from the shadows, steps the same figure.

You: (In shock) Ya, you . . . you're . . . you're.

He whips a glaring, stainless, silver 9mm pistol out, with an engraved word that reads as *choices*. Then he rests the barrel on your forehead.

You: . . . You're . . . me.

The assailant (You): *And you're fired . . .*

Bang!

That is until you wake up. Your eyes spring open. You: *It was. . . only a dream!*

You: *Mike, Pat . . . Dad! Mom! Wait, was Betty-Grandma? Was Dad there because of his strong financial support? Was mom there because of her constant hands on help? Was grandma there because of her senior- level approval?*

Are these the people I'm really working for?

You get up. You look deeply into the mirror as you prepare for work with the sole motive for working being either the fear of not having money or the greed of having more. So while staring into the doorways to your soul, you ask yourself . . .

"Who. Do. You. Work. For?"

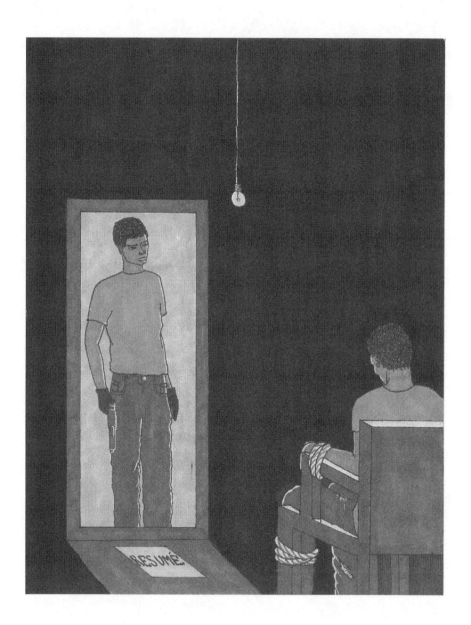

What's Up? Talk to Me!   Who Do You Work For?

Are you working somewhere you want to work? Are you working in your job solely for the money?

Does it feel temporary or permanent?

Do you have a dream job or career in mind?

Does it involve creating a position for yourself or applying for one? Either is fine as long as you're happy there!

I saw a post somewhere online that said, "If you're not working for your dream, you're working for someone else's." Are you in your position because you chose or someone chose for you?

---

www.thecmwexperience.com

Check out the blog section of the book's website for the full experience.

Your Why

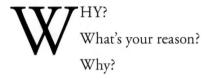WHY?
What's your reason?
Why?

What fuels you?

Why?

What gives you purpose?

A tree's source of life is its roots.

Without them, it could not continue.

What is your deep-rooted reason?

A flame is not ablaze without its fuel.

So what are your actions without purpose?

You're never limited to one *why*, but

You are limited, without at least one *why*.

You live life going through the motions, aimlessly following a routine.

Aimlessly drifting in the wind without direction

And without a strong desire.

Beginning days with no drive and no expectations for the day

Or even the future.

Or . . .

There are activities, events, or even goals you can embark on,

Yet, there is always some sort of conundrum that appears.

Activities become mundane and pointless.

Events become lackluster and long.

Goals become distant and waver.

This could all derive from the *lack of* a *why* or *a why that's not Strong enough.*

Your *why* is the third voice that tells you to get up!

Whether that is getting up out of bed after your body has been

Infused with the mattress or getting up off the floor once life has

Slammed you on your back.

Your *why* tells you things like:

Keep going!

You can because you must!

You can because you're supposed to!

You have someone depending on you!

You have people believing in you!

You have people saying you won't and can't!

You owe it to yourself!

Your *why* for working out and going to work

May have two different levels of depth.

Regardless of how deep or shallow your reason for doing so is,

There always needs to be a *why*.

The *why* can be "because it makes me happy,"

"Because I want what's best for my future," or

"Because there are lives depending on me."

Just know it. If you know it, you can focus on it.

If you focus on it, you give purpose to your life.

So why do you wake up every day? What is your why?

What's Up? Talk to Me! Your Why

What is your why (purpose)?

Are you satisfied with your why?

Who does it involve or majorly affect?

---

www.thecmwexperience.com

Check out the blog section of the book's website for the full experience.

Undergrad Cheat Sheet

G ROWTH ONLY ENDS when your time does.
So we're never truly done with this perpetual process of progression, even in old age.

No one has all the answers,

And there is not one universal answer that works for every single person. Consequently, no one can tell you how to live your life,

But I can make suggestions.

Perspective is key. From a given angle, a specific number can be viewed a six or nine. Your perception and interpretation is what forms your reality. From one to nine, which would you rather see? How do you see yourself?

- "Why not me?"—Question your current reality. Question the obstacles, limitations, and circumstances keeping you from what you want and where you want to be. Why can't you . . . ? Then realize that most, if not all, of your answers are actually excuses you conjured up. There is no reason it can't be you who is healthy, wealthy, happy, etc.

- "I will"—Speak into your future. This is an affirmation to your prosperous future. Speak audaciously to the position you will claim.

- "I am"—Know and believe the greatness you possess. Speaking this is establishing and claiming what you want because it's already being planted inside of you. We have so much untapped and unexplored potential within us. This is saying you've found yours.

Law of attraction. Whatever you feed energy, believe in, and focus on is what you give life to, is what gravitates toward you, and is what becomes part of your environment. Though it may not be sudden, the proof will be evident. It may be something minor that relates to your grand desire or just something generally positive. If positive, that's what you are attracting. Be mindful that negativity only breeds negativity.

Faith. With faith comes hope. Believing in yourself and your higher power creates faith. Then, moving by faith and not by sight creates strength. By not being moved by circumstances, situations, and stipulations that are hindering you, the shackles of doubt are removed. Move forward with the latent beast inside that reminds you that there is greater in store for you and greatness inside of you. That is, if you believe so.

Time and place. "There is a time and place for everything." I interpret this as balance. There is a time and place for the following: time for yourself vs. time for others, struggle vs. breakthrough, speaking vs. listening, vacation vs. work. It seems like common sense, but at times, we forget to enjoy the lives we have worked so hard for. At times, we forget that even in the bad, some good things can come out of it or follow it. Bring balance to your life, but at times, the balance you bring to the table could be what tips the scale in others' unbalanced lives.

The Golden Rule (treat others how you would want to be treated). Known but forgotten . . . or just not applied. Place yourself in their soles and tread the terrain you placed them in. It's easy to forget to try to see things from their perspective when your first priority is *I*. However, regardless of what the situation may be, at times, applying the Golden Rule is as simple as trying to understand. Whether that understanding is in the how, the why, or the who, it makes all the difference. Application of the Golden Rule is also seen by simply assisting a little. Things like giving while knowing you may not receive anything in return, whether to family or to a stranger.

Optimize with optimism. First, create the optimism by locating the bright side. The *bright side* seems like a cliché, yet that does not make it any less important. It is a factor that multiplies a positive outlook in a situation. Find it by asking, how could this be beneficial? What good could come from this? It takes an open mind and a strong will with the desire to overcome. It takes crashing the pity party. It takes confidence in yourself to see what blessings your future holds. This is how you optimize with optimism; you make the most of the situation. To optimize your optimism, you need the gateway drug. That drug is a sense of humor. Laugher is a medication, and yet it's contagious. If you could learn to laugh more, you could learn to live longer.

Love you. Be sure to love yourself because you should not move on to the next section without doing so first. How can you give something you never had for yourself?

You're the author behind the story, the cartographer behind the path, And architect behind the blueprint.

Yet the finished product is not done until you are.

Your job is to construct, formulate, and spawn a life worth living.

A life worth remembering.

What's Up? Talk to Me!   Undergrad Cheat Sheet

Check it out! Before you continue, I just wanted to be the first to say . . . well, turn the page!

www.thecmwexperience.com

Check out the blog section of the book's website for the full experience.

Congrats! You've been awarded your Bachelor's in Growth.

The University of Life

THE FACULTY OF THE UNIVERSITY OF LIFE
HEREBY ADMIT

TO THE DEGREE OF

Growth Degree

Bachelor of Achievement in Growth

God

President Of The University of Life

Carl M. Watson

Dean Of The College

Welcome to the Graduate Level

Our Master's in Love Journey

LEARNING OBJECTIVES IN LOVE

Graduate Syllabus

THIS SECTION IS the revealing of an entire different world. What is in the undergrad section can be applied in some of the coming areas. However, it is more than feasible to have skipped the undergrad section in order to enjoy this one. The difference between the sections lie in the topics and how the information is conveyed. I will not simply state what I suggest could or should be done. I will not spell out what the lesson is. Instead, my adventure will become your captivating journey. I will share experiences, moments, and perspectives. Some pieces will actually prompt questions for you. This will be a more hands on self-study. What I will do is provide you with moments that everyone has or will experience at some point. I will provide you with curiosity, disappointment, joy, *aw* moments, familiarity but most importantly, I will provide you with entertainment.

This section is not here to define rights and wrongs about love, but it is intended to help you formulate your own answers. Note that not every piece is written with the same style. Also, while this is written from a male's perspective, all can relate. Before you embark on this journey, I challenge you as you read to find or create the positive within the negative endings. I pray you find one that resonates with you, one you wholeheartedly connect with. Again, I ask that as you relate, you record those moments in each piece. Be sure to be attentive to the transition from the dark abyss known as heartache to the sanguine outlook of love realized once it's found. Don't be alarmed by the raw emotions captured in the beginning. In fact, as a treat, I will start us with something that originally came later in the curriculum. With that being said, welcome!

The Digits Chase

I T WASN'T MY first time seeing her, just the first time I spoke to her. We were in the library. I was apprehensive, and bullied by Fear. Yet there is always someone bigger and scarier, and in this case, his name was Regret. I thought of lines smoother than a baby's bottom dipped in butter, sliding across ice. What came out was just a simple icebreaker—"Hey, do you have a pencil?"—while a well-concealed writing utensil lay in my pocket. However, the words of this casual conversation passed like stray bullets in a standoff . . . within seconds, it was over. A battle lost, not a lost war.

I saw her again, in the same location, different day, and she was a friend of a friend. It could have been my imagination or a sixth sense, but there were bright signs hovering over the both of them. The signs, with enough lights to celebrate Christmas every day, which said, "Go, stupid." My friend was her friend, so her friend was my friend. Now we had a connection. Now we studied together . . . as a group. I got to see the brains behind the beauty. And just like that, she had it. Like a ghost, I could not see her coming, but it was in her possession now. She had it; she had my attention. Like a newborn who wouldn't stop crying, she had my attention.

However, that was the very reason I was afraid to get those seven digits that would enable a conversation at any time. Digits that would defy the effects of time. They were the keys needed to open the door to a connection to someone.

I returned to my second home, the library. I found her (as if I wasn't looking). We conversed on a more personal level. In this interaction, I intended to fish for information but found sunken treasure. Wait, no, she couldn't be. She couldn't be funny. She couldn't be driven.

She couldn't be noble and kind. She couldn't always be in the library. She couldn't be . . . what I had been looking for. This opinionated, intellectual left me without a choice. I had to get those seven digits. These digits would create a connection that would be better than Wi-Fi.

Slap! Right in my face! The word hit me, leaving a mark of disappointment. "No." Yet she was not pushing me away. I left in a state similar to that of a turtle on a highway (hurt and confused). We connected as if the library was a hot spot, so why say such a hurtful word? She said she didn't know me that well, but how else do you get to know someone? Is a bird born flying? Are we birthed sprinting out of the womb? It was not automatic, and this was how we take steps out of uncertainty.

Another battle lost, but another opportunity presented itself a day or two later. Same location, but different results. With comedy as my wrecking ball, I slowly tore down her walls of doubt. Smiles and a playful attitude surrounded us. I stayed longer than intended just for the opportunity to (*cough, cough* study) ask again. We happened to leave at the same time. I walked her to her car, her books in my hand. We arrived at the car and began talking as if we had been friends for years. With fire in my eyes and confidence in everything I said, I asked again.

Me: "How do you get to know someone if you are unable to communicate?"

Her: "We see each other in the library every day or every other day."
Me: "Exactly, we've gotten to know each other, but I don't want to keep interrupting your studying. This way I can get to know you better when we're not both busy."

Well, something along those lines, and then something smooth thrown in—followed by something funny to repel her slick rebuttal. Finally, with a sigh and beautiful smile, I was given those digits that became a doorway to a dream. I say that because this was how I got to know my dream girl . . . at least, that's what I thought.

What's Up? Talk to Me!   The Digits Chase

Share your creativity with me. What's the most creative way you've gotten someone's number or attention?

_____

What were the results?

_____

_____

_____

www.thecmwexperience.com

Check out the blog section of the book's website for the full experience.

The Investor

I SIT . . . I sit, pondering this feeling. What is this feeling?
As if there is a void, a black hole is swallowing my joy.
Is this . . . loneliness,

Or is it sorrow?

I sit here thinking of all the time I gave you,

All the time you borrowed.

Like a bank, I must charge you interest

Because my interest in you has grown with time.

I sit here with hopes that you would return what I have invested.

But as expected . . . you don't.

And maybe you won't.

But who am I?

Who am I, but a lonely investor of time, affection, joy, and comfort?

However, you assure me that this does not fit into the budget;

Not the budget of someone of your stature.

You want someone who drives something faster,

. . . But I have a BMW.

You want someone who looks dapper,

. . . But my closet is entirely polo; you've never seen such a stable.

No, no, no!

You want someone more like a rapper,

. . . But I have a wider diction, better dance moves, and more ambition.

Oh, I see, you want a bad boy. No, no, no!

You want disaster,

But all I can offer is security.

What's Up? Talk to Me! The Investor

Ladies: Have you ever gone through a bad-boy phase? What was one of your worst bad-boy phase experiences you've encountered?

_____

Fellas: Have you ever gone through a nice-guy phase? What was one of your worst nice-guy phase experiences you encountered?

_____

Have you ever been friendzoned? Tell me about it. Have you friendzoned someone purposely?

_____

You know you can't just say yes and not share, right? Was it to actually be friends or to create space?

_____

_____

_____

www.thecmwexperience.com

Check out the blog section of the book's website for the full experience.

Prescribed

I SIT WITH NOTHING to drown my pain in,
As if something other than you could relieve it.
Pain caused by loneliness
Because I can't find that miss
. . . "Miss Right."
I need you, if even just for one night.
But when you leave in the morning, the pain would only return.
So maybe I need you for a day.
A little bit of happiness a day keeps the loneliness away.
But I don't want temporary happiness.
I want eternal joy.
The only prescription the doctor prescribes is a daily dose of you.
But apparently, this is not something you can find at your local pharmacy
Because it is so hard to find you.
Where could you be?
So, I just use what I can find at my local pharmacies,
But all I achieve
Is the knowledge that no one else can relieve,
This pain!
Now I feel like I'm going insane
Because I continue to do the same things.
Visiting these local pharmacies,
Now all I've received are the side effects from these generic brands

Because there's no substitute for you.

Now I suffer from a broken heart, low expectations, high hopes,

And crushed dreams.

I may be losing my mind!

But if I could ever get this prescription filled,

Maybe I'll find my heart.

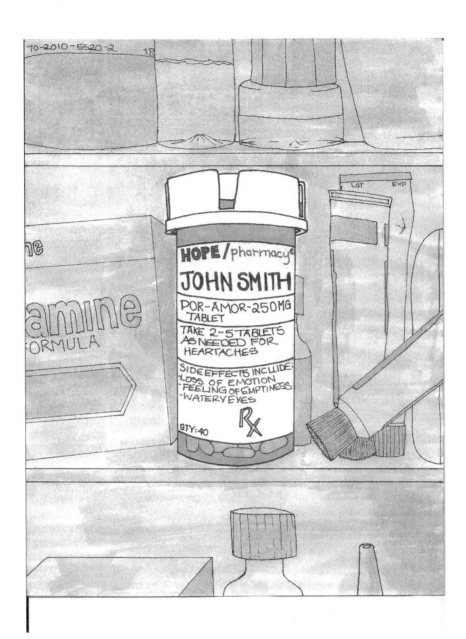

What's Up? Talk to Me!   Prescribed

This is one of those lonely night moments. Sometimes I get carried away when writing in the moment, but it only lasts for the moment.

What goes through your mind on nights like that?

How do you or how could you pull yourself up to keep from drowning in your feelings?

---

www.thecmwexperience.com

Check out the blog section of the book's website for the full experience.

The Longest Smile

TRUTH IS, I fail to understand this attraction to you.
For some reason, I gravitate toward you
Without an inkling or a clue.
Could it be your voice that creates this possible fatal attraction?
. . . A voice that fills the air with joy.
As soon as it hits my ear, it penetrates my heart
Because suddenly, I'm overcome and happy.

Or could it be your native tongue,
Which seems like a foreign language to me.
The language known as sarcasm that you speak so clearly.
It irritates me while simultaneously
Making me smile.
It keeps me on my toes, and it keeps me interested.

But the real reason I stay, If I may,
Is your smile, which is the highlight of my day. Maybe,
Because when I see it, I feel it has lightened the way
To your heart.

It could be your athleticism that I hope, can match mine.
Gymnastics and volleyball, huh?

Yet the attraction is more than physical.

Your optimism can be inspiring at times.

The consistent smiles seem to continue for miles.

Until the point that I can't really tell when you are having a bad day.

You know how to create a good time,

As if it were your very own blueprint.

You're the ray of shine most people pray they wake up to . . .

And now it's the reason I smile too.

What's Up? Talk to Me!   The Longest Smile

Have you ever ran into someone, who was always sarcastic, yet always happy and smiling (not quite the rude, condescending sarcasm)?

_____

What was it like?

_____

No? Oh, well, I have and I really hope that you get the chance to meet someone similar.

_____

_____

_____

www.thecmwexperience.com

Check out the blog section of the book's website for the full experience.

Bless You

HOW? HOW DID I allow this to happen again?
I thought I was taking my "F-love" vitamins daily.
I began to show symptoms early.
After only a few encounters, I was coughing up "what-ifs?"
What if we were together?
What if she doesn't like me?
What if I have nothing to say?
What if she's the one?
. . . What?
What if . . . what if I don't get control of my thoughts?
A head cold caused by thoughts of her.
Sneezing out excess compliments.
Looking for tissues in order to clear my sinuses.
Maybe I should use a roll of reality
Maybe I should use a roll of past disappointments.
No, that's too rough for my nose,
But how did it happen?
Was there just some love in the air and I inhaled a little too much?
I guess I caught some feelings.
And to no surprise, did the negative effect take place.
Heartache, headache, and sadness occur in no particular order.
Such a deadly sickness can be life-threatening if not treated properly.
Tests have shown that after each case of the sickness that I catch,

My heart gets weaker.

A morning dose of prayer is used to remove the sickness, but

Not the pain.

The pain is embedded in the cortex,

As if deposited into the memory banks.

Be careful because some who are infected can hide the effects,

And no one would know.

It's very contagious in a generation of situationships.

Maybe I just thought she was the cure.

What's Up? Talk to Me!   Bless You

Have you ever been caught off guard by a subtle attraction when you weren't looking for it?

_____

What happened that made you realize you were attracted to the person?

_____

How does the story go?

_____

If this doesn't apply to you, I'll catch you on the next page.

_____

_____

_____

www.thecmwexperience.com

Check out the blog section of the book's website for the full experience.

The Math

ONE IS THE loneliest number.
And two heads are better than one.
Three is definitely a crowd.
So I guess the perfect number is two,
Me and you.
One plus one equals two.
Isn't that what we're taught at an early age?
I count as one person,
And *you* count as one person.
Together we make two; it was already set in stone.
I realized my joy is amplified when you're here.
So when you're around, my happiness is squared.
But what about when you leave my side and disappear
For more than two seconds,
I feel as though I'm divided in half,
But in reality, I'm stuck at one—the lonely number.
When I hang out with my friend and his number two,
All I can think of is you.
I sit there as the third wheel.
So to keep myself busy, I search for something.
Something, I feel I am missing . . . some missing variable.

And I know it's something valuable,

Like the value of x.

Then I see you with a smile on your face,

And I realize it's you.

What could be more valuable?

What's Up? Talk to Me! The Math

Do you know how many math classes an engineer has to take?

It's not important, just something to lighten the mood. This was one I wrote just for entertainment.

I hope you were feeling it and enjoyed it.

---

www.thecmwexperience.com

Check out the blog section of the book's website for the full experience.

A Numbers Game

YOU THOUGHT YOU found the one,
But you're not the only one, trying to be the only one.
"Cool, I'll settle for number one!"

One of . . . ? How many?

Do you include her friends, the exes, the day-to-day randoms,

The "oh, he's cutes" or the best friends?

That's 1, 2, 3 . . . 4 . . . 10 . . . out of fingers and outnumbered,

But unbothered.

How many times has this ratio appeared?

In every encounter,

How can you be so sure?

No one is ever completely depleted of options.

Some just choose not to acknowledge them.

We are simply counting the ones we want but don't have or can't have.

A closet full of clothes, but nothing to wear.

A fridge with food to cook, but nothing to eat.

A television with a variety of stations, but nothing to watch.

A computer with a plethora of songs, yet nothing to listen to.

However, you only need one.

Did you find her?

Maybe, but you only get one time to make a first impression.

You only need one . . .

Authentic one-on-one encounter, one date, one time to hang out.

Then one smile . . . the first one.

It's the beautiful beacon that signifies that the ice has been broken.

Now you swim in their personality,

And try not to drown in your own feelings.

So now there's two . . . wait, no . . . there's three.

Your mind: recalling good and bad memories, analyzing what they say with their mouth and body, having irrelevant thoughts and feelings.

Wait, no . . . the feelings come from a fourth party.

Your heart: "This one here." "This again?" "Cool, let's try one more time!"

What's funny is maybe the use of *one*

Triggered thoughts of that one person or that one moment.

I just hope the numbers play in your favor.

What's Up? Talk to Me!   A Numbers Game

What's one first impression you made that you will never forget?

_____

What are two first impressions others made that you will never forget?
What are three reasons why you love this book and will keep reading?

_____

I'm joking, unless you take it seriously. Your choice.

_____

_____

_____

www.thecmwexperience.com

Check out the blog section of the book's website for the full experience.

Treasure

H AVE I FOUND it?
   Have I found what most men scour the world for?
   There's nothing I want more.
Its value exceeds that of
A house, a car, a jet, even a star.
It's something within reach,
Yet further away than a new galaxy.
. . . Is this what entices a man to search?
The funny thing is,
This search can become a great blessing and a minor curse,
But most continue once they understand its worth.
This treasure some men actually find,
But never realize until it is lost to them.
Some men find it, preserve it, appreciate it,
And flourish because of it.
Some don't even know what the treasure is, but they continue to search.
But I know!
It's a heart of gold,
It's priceless,
And can never be sold.
(But for my sake, maybe it can be stolen.)
It comes with a smile that shines brighter than the sun.
Words more valuable than a jewel because they produce

Greater smiles, more joy, and close open wounds.

Yet a tongue sharper than a harpoon

Used to take down great whites.

Blessed with beauty!

Beauty that even a goddess couldn't attain.

To me, its something treasured for more than just one night.

The problem is being deceived by fool's gold.

What's Up? Talk to Me! Treasure

What are some characteristics in someone you treasure?

_____

Who are some people you treasure?

_____

Do you show or tell them? It goes a long way if you do so sporadically, even if it's a feeling that's already understood.

_____

If you have identified the one you treasure, you cannot do one without doing the other, that is show them and not tell them how you feel. It doesn't work like that! Do both – show and tell them even if you struggle with expressing how you feel, especially, the fellas because I have been there. Try it, or you may end up with a lot of unanswered questions.

_____

_____

_____

www.thecmwexperience.com

Check out the blog section of the book's website for the full experience.

The Meeting

ANGER SAYS, "F**K it. F**K it all."
Peace thinks of a better way.
Sadness is left with nothing to say,
With nothing but negativity accumulating like a rolling snowball.
Sadness confides in Anger.
Peace begins to slowly fall victim to his own anger; with nothing to say,
He hits a wall.
It only gets worse.
Peace says, "I cannot support these ideas nor will I."
Anger taps Sadness and says,
"Maybe those memories will help him pick a side."
Sadness has only documented memories of pain.
He slides them across the brain.
Just when it seems that Anger has struck a nerve,
And Peace's ideas have begun to curve,
Good walks in, also known as the
God in Me, the Good Guy, and the Golden Path.
With no words and a small smirk, he lays across the table
Nothing but documented joyful memories.
Memories not limited by the pain of the past,
Also known as failed encounters.
"Why not just get rid of the heart?" mumbles Sadness.
Peace and Good simultaneously sprout up and shout,

"Because we'd remove love and our uniqueness!"

As if a spark had been lit, Anger explodes.

He slams his fist onto the brain and yells,

"No, we remove our weaknesses!"

Then Love kicks in the door.

Known for his kindness and feared for his passion,

With flames in his eyes,

He shouts about the extraction.

Yet to everyone's surprise, he offers a great compromise.

Love says, "Keep half of the heart.

The half that holds love for family and friends."

"Remove the half that holds love for companionship."

"The half that's constantly under construction."

"The half that will soon . . . fail to function."

What's Up? Talk to Me!   The Meeting

If you've been sharing your story with me thus far, I feel like I can share more of mine.

Have you ever become acquainted with someone and shortly after, you begin hanging out with them on a more intimate (but not physical) level? As their love life becomes more active, you simultaneously find out how active it was and how physically intimate it is becoming. Living and enjoying life is one thing, but it's important to be discreet about your business. Now that you know, you choose to stop hanging out on that same level with the same interest. Here's the funny part—the person starts dating the friend you used to bring around sometimes, when visiting them. I know it's a tad specific, but have you experienced something somewhat similar? If so, tell your story.

_____

_____

_____

www.thecmwexperience.com

Check out the blog section of the book's website for the full experience.

Forbidden Fruit

I PUT ON THIS facade, as if her presence doesn't create an expectation for each day. As if I don't have my heart set on the daily sample of this forbidden fruit. A smile that manipulates my own smile, as if it is tugging at the corners of my lips and forcing them upward. Yet like the sun behind the clouds that still shines, on the surface, the smile may not appear. However, behind the surface, there is a smile brighter than the sun. They say no one person should have too much power. Then how is it that she does? Intelligence, ambition, beauty, charisma, and developed—so much power in one individual. Yet at times, she still doesn't understand her full value, like an amazing surprise gift with no price tag. I can tell her, but I would much rather show her. That's where the problem lies. Like Adam and Eve, I cannot have this fruit. Out of respect for the relationship that brings her joy, I create distance. Like two positive charges that could never connect, which is only a negative situation for me. However, I'm complacent with a friendship because it is a bittersweet feeling of never fully being there, but never fully being gone. The distance I create is more so for me so that it is easier for me to see the line between friendship and "complicated." This way, I only visit the garden when I need to. I just admire her power, this fruit, from a distance.

What's Up? Talk to Me!   Forbidden Fruit

Was there a time in your life where circumstances wouldn't allow you to be more than friends with someone—things such as being in a relationship, complicating a work relationship, or jeopardizing something that was already mutually beneficial?

_____

What stopped you?

_____

What was the better route (friends or something more), and would you change things if you could?

_____

In my case, things worked out better with us as friends.

_____

_____

_____

www.thecmwexperience.com

Check out the blog section of the book's website for the full experience.

No

YOU CONVINCE YOURSELF, "What's the worst she can say,
No?"
When you realize your biggest fear is
Just a simple two-letter word,
The sharp rocks along this dark path smoothens out as you begin to go.
The sides along the path illuminate
With a few flickers of fear and temptation.
You see it! You feel it!
Here is the opportunity!
Now is where you take control and, with both hands,
Take hold of the wheel.
Now seize the opportunity to go in for the kill.
Words produced like combos, creating a combination compiled of
Actions, locations, adjectives, and adverbs to form a question.
Yet in a split second . . .
A response . . . "no," counters faster than an eye could process.
"Finish him."
It leaves one knife in my head and the other in my chest. So in just two blows,
And she did it all with only . . . a *no.*
But I guess wounds only hurt for so long . . .
Because *yes* will be there before you know.

Allow me to be a little biased here. Most women—nearly all—are the ones being approached. I say it with love, but I don't feel like ladies fully grasp how much confidence it takes to approach a woman you're truly interested in. It's like being trapped in a room full of people with a bomb in it. I can write the word *bomb* in my own book, right? Anyway, you sum up enough confidence to decide to be the hero and volunteer to disarm it. Now you must choose your wires carefully instead of using instinct. Who knows, the bomb could be in a bad mood and blow up anyway.

Whether you are a guy or a lady (much respect if this pertains to you), tell me what was the worst rejection you have experienced.

How did you or how could you have recover(ed) from it?

www.thecmwexperience.com

Check out the blog section of the book's website for the full experience.

The Result

I AM TRULY BLESSED,
But stressed at best.
I lend a hand.

I lend an ear.

I lend my heart,

But it's treated like forsaken pieces of undesired trash.

All along,

I have emitted fumes.

I guess love is in the air,

But you hold your breath in fear of feeling:

B eyond

E xtraordinary

A mazing

U nique

T rusted

I rreplaceable

F un

U nited

L oved

You fail to realize that I'm not here to kill,

But to give life to true joy – your happiness.

Yet with only a few pieces of my heart remaining,

I'm focusing on keeping the rest locked away.

I try to give what most women spend their life searching for,

But at this point, I have lost the key.

And I'm not even looking for it.

Maybe you can find it, but if you do Don't return it!

What's Up? Talk to Me!   The Result

I had a few creative rejections that inspired this. For example, back-and-forth texting and speaking. Suddenly, without warning, everything stops one day. Then the following day or so, while out and about, I see her standing next to a guy, talking to people. Our eyes lock. Then she looks away and proceeds to quickly grab the guy's arm and hand. Followed by a kiss to make sure there was no confusion on my part, I'm assuming. What's crazy is that there was still a little confusion . . . imagine that. Mainly because there was never any mention of a boyfriend in any of our conversations.

What's a creative way you have seen, heard, or experienced rejection?

---

www.thecmwexperience.com

Check out the blog section of the book's website for the full experience.

Shadow Eyes

S HE'S SHY.
She seems to prefer the shadows
With no desire to be in the limelight.
Her connection with attention is similar to that of a cat and water.
However, her strut demands attention, as does a model's catwalk.
There is no difference between the two.
Beauty such as hers should be a crime to hide from the world,
But there is one thing she can't hide . . .those eyes.
Whether in the shadows, in a crowd, or in her habitat,
A gorgeous hazel pair of jewels, with the ability to paralyze all thoughts.
Fluent in her own language, known to most as sarcasm.
Blessed with a talent to create masterpieces.
How and why she remains in the shadows
Baffles me.
With the image of those eyes burned into my memories,
Even in the shadows, I noticed her.
She has my attention, but what she'll do with it, is as unknown
As the shadows.

How would you bring a shy individual out of their shell on a first date?

_____

If you're someone who is shy or more conservative, how would you like to be approached and interacted with?

_____

_____

_____

www.thecmwexperience.com

Check out the blog section of the book's website for the full experience.

The Summer Greek

WHEN EXAMINING A box,
One always inquires about its contents.
No matter the beauty of the exterior,
Its true value is not discovered until the interior is explored.
A book's cover is simply the book's advertisement, and its pages are
The movie.
It was the summer.
At first glance, the eyes admire. The legs follow, but the mind rushes.
Yet, the heart remains in the shadows behind bars, but not for too long.
Words exchanged as if they were currency, as if it was bail.
She's so noble, a hero of the young,
As if the calling was embedded in her DNA.
Such ambition,
Such fire.
Enough to fuel a locomotive.
Enough on her plate to feed a family of five.
To balance such positions of power, responsibility, and devotion,
The greatest circus has never seen such a juggling act.
I've realized the value inside.
She is known as Cutie when wearing her pink and green
AKA
Goofy
AKA

Joyful

AKA

Kind

Also known as

. . . To be announced.

What's Up? Talk to Me!   The Summer Greek

Do you know about Greek life?

_____

If you are not Greek, as a young adult, would you date a Greek? Of course, I would need you to tell me why.

_____

If you are Greek, as a young adult, would you date a Greek? Why?

_____

_____

_____

www.thecmwexperience.com

Check out the blog section of the book's website for the full experience.

Nervous

SHE SEEMS ALMOST a little unreal,
As if not of this planet.
But she is so down-to-earth.
Someone I'm comfortable around,
Yet thinking of her makes me nervous.
What could I possibly be afraid of?
Her smile?
How open-minded she is?
Her ambition?
Her athleticism?
Her beauty?
Her booty?
Well, that's not it.
Maybe it's the fact that she has a child,
Which does not negate her assets.
If anything, it enhances them.
Could it be my fear of nourishing a life before mine is established?
Yet, I still want to know more about this little Hercules.
Hmm, that's only the beginning.
She seems to like me as much as I like her.
But key word being *seems*.
I cannot seem to see clearly through these glasses because
They have been scratched by the pain of the past.

My past continues to whisper to me, saying,

"Keep your guard up until I give you the signal."

I don't even know what I want.

I just know God has the answer.

But while I wait for His reply, I ask my heart.

It may seem too soon to even talk to this guy, but

He usually has the answers.

It seems even he is stuck between what my brain says and

What he was made for.

That . . . that makes me nervous!

Brain: I am tired of these reruns! I already know how this ends, the same way it always does.

Heart: Well, I'm not looking for love yet . . . I think. I just want a connection for now . . . I think. I want to see what's out there . . . I think.

Brain: Well, stop thinking so much. Thinking is what got you hurt last time. Just leave the thinking to me!

Heart: I know I still have God, family, friends, school, and basketball!

So I think we should be good . . . I hope.

What's Up? Talk to Me!   Nervous

Would you date someone with a child while both of you were in your twenties? Why or Why not?

_____

How would things change if the age range was in your thirties?

_____

If you have had that experience, how did it work out?

_____

_____

_____

www.thecmwexperience.com

Check out the blog section of the book's website for the full experience.

The Separation for Survival

SOMETHING I HAVE always dreaded
. . . Being on the other side,
Being the one to pull the trigger.
However, my situation differs
From others in my opinion
Because I'm doing this for the nation.
The nation of me and, ironically, the nation of we.
It's either her or me,
But of course, I hesitate to pull the trigger,
And release the bullet of rejection.
. . . Open wounds that release nothing but sorrow.
The worst part is that I am no stranger to the other side of the barrel.
I could lay down my arms and allow my nation to suffer
While simultaneously going through the motions and become
Depleted of its resources:
Like time, money, energy, and more importantly, joy.
The nation of we is directly affected by both the nation of she and me.
So if the nation of me cannot fully invest resources such as time and
Joy, then the nation of we cannot be.

Because that's what the nation of we deserves and needs.
From the nation of me emerged thoughts of a friendship and a treaty.
However, the nation of she initiated the action,

Which resulted in her dissatisfaction.

By the hands of she, the treaty was nullified.

For the nations of me and she to flourish, the nation of we

Would meet its demise,

And the pistol of truth is the only way.

It would be like two birds, who each had one wing tied to one another.

Both are flapping their opposing wings, same speed and direction,

Both birds can get to their destination together;

However, when one bird begins to flap slower

And fly in a different direction, both birds are affected,

So the ties must be severed.

It is all the separation for survival.

What's Up? Talk to Me!   The Separation for Survival

We're friends here! Tell me, have you been dating, been talking to, or been in a relationship with someone, but you were both on different levels of interest or investment? Consequently, was it better for everyone if you both separated?

_____

Can you share your story?

_____

_____

_____

www.thecmwexperience.com

Check out the blog section of the book's website for the full experience.

The Approach

H ER PRESENCE CAUSES
The metal detectors to go off, the alarms grab your ears.
The eyes gravitate toward her with this magnetic attraction.

The legs frozen.

The heart rushing.

The mind . . .

Blank . . . no, it flickers.

A smile so genuine,

So heartwarming,

So . . . right.

Her beauty is equal to none other.

Minor words exchanged, but time well spent.

My only regret . . . is not having the opportunity to spend it all on her.

Her physique represents the miles, laps, and times

She ran through my mind.

How is it that she's so close but seems so far out of my reach?

I'm drunk off the image of her displayed on social media.

As if I'm under the influence . . . her influence.

(R)adiant

(A)ttractive

(V)ibrant

(E)loquent

(N)ow . . .

Is always the right time to approach her.

What's Up? Talk to Me!   The Approach

What is the most elaborate approach you or someone you know has come up with to approach someone they were into?

_____

_____

_____

www.thecmwexperience.com

Check out the blog section of the book's website for the full experience.

Rated M for Mature

I LIKE TO PLAY around and even play with words to get to your Heart.

But I would never try to play with your heart.

See, I'm fairly new to this game; I didn't get it on its release date.

It wasn't until college that I got my copy of it because

I've always been a rookie (AKA flirt) in another game,

On a smaller scale.

Lots of times, I don't even like to play it;

School occupies most of my time anyway.

Yet, everyone gets their copy at some point, it seems.

I dove in headfirst. Now rules read, and no created player made.

It took some time, but I slowly learned the core rules of the game,

And the players involved.

Rule #1. In this game (and in this generation), no one is ever fully yours. They're like a paycheck. You know ahead of time how much to expect (100 percent), but once you receive it, you later find that someone else has possession of a percentage of it too. It occurs wherever you receive your paycheck and wherever you play. But where in the settings can I change this?

Rule #2. Never erase all your characters for that one special unlocked character until you are sure the character is unlocked. However, if it is Player 2 that you want . . . still *do not* erase all your characters to get her. If you do, you have violated Rule #2 because you didn't understand Rule #1 (happened to me plenty of times).

"Who are these characters, and who is Player 2?" you may ask.

Characters. These are those who you flirt with here and there in the game. You may text now and then. They're cool to be around, but there is nothing serious between you two. You wouldn't fight a boss battle with a character . . . well, not as often as with a Player 2.

Boss battle. These are those life obstacles and hardships we all have to go through. They vary from needing a ride from work and needing an ear to vent to losing a job to losing a loved one.

Player 2. Discovering Player 2 was such a shock to me. This is why I should have read the rules and played the tutorial. Player 2 always seemed like a victim in the media, in society, and in my eyes. The one who always ends up heartbroken? Player 2 is "her or she," the woman. The one that has the majority of your attention; the one you really want. More importantly, Player 2 is usually better, more cunning, more deceiving, and more nefarious. Why, you may ask? Player 2's settings are different in this game (i.e., settings - double standards). Player 2 has this special ability where even when she is wrong, despite logical settings, "she's right." Player 2 also has the ability to make herself the victim despite being the villain. Player 2 usually has more unlocked characters than Player 1. This is because the majority of the time, Player 2 does not have to try to unlock characters. Due to their different settings, characters are just unlocked for them over time.

So I customize my character accordingly, but I still, at times,

End up losing to Player 2

By deleting characters and not playing the game like other Player 1s would.

Yet, I'm not the type to attack Player 2

With my sword and shield then leave (think about it).

I don't play this game for the heck of it.

I don't want to injure Player 2—consequently turning her play style into

Something more aggressive and cold.

I just want to beat the game and turn Player 2 into the *One.*

Yet every time I feel like I'm about to beat the game

. . . I lose and must hit Restart.

What's Up? Talk to Me! Rated M for Mature

What are some rules or tips you would provide to your past self about dating when in college?

_____

How about some rules or tips when in your twenties?

_____

How would those rules change (if at all) when in your thirties and older?

_____

_____

_____

www.thecmwexperience.com

Check out the blog section of the book's website for the full experience.

The High School Crush

THE TRUTH IS, even if I did not show it much,
Since the day we met, I've had a crush.
However, the problem with a crush is
The result of sharing your feelings.
You built up these hopes that the other person feels the same way
You do.
Just to have the plane of reality crash into your building of hope,
And all that remains is what's left of you buried beneath the rubble.
The idea of this happening to me created chains of fear
Until I realized the key was in your smile. The smile after my jokes,
The smile after a compliment, even a smile when you were mad
Or even sad.

I begin to feel complacent with what we had.
Yet with time came new admirers for you and me.
But at the end of the tunnel, it was still you I would see.
Truthfully, I wanted to take you to the prom,
But I backed out of the race.
It wasn't until I saw him kiss your face
That I realized I came in last place. Now what are we . . .
Friends?

I do know what *you* are though.

You are a beautiful woman with a bright future.

I'm sure you'll leave your stamp on history regardless of what

Your career path may be.

A Kanye fan

But beneath

A Rihanna fan

But beneath

A great smile

But beneath

A kind heart

But beneath

Ambition so strong it burns holes in glaciers.

But beneath that . . .

You are and can be whatever you set your mind to.

And I believe that, I truly do.

But this must have been an intricate chess game

Since you waited half a decade to make your move.

Now your newly revealed feelings for me have me taken aback.

So do you picture us together when we're near?

Is this Snapchat?

Because I posted the same picture,

But over time, mine disappeared.

What's Up? Talk to Me!   The High School Crush

Have you ever had a crush on someone and later down the line, the roles changed – the crushee now becomes the crusher? Did you feel the same way as you once did? Did you give it a chance?

_____

What do think caused their change of heart?

_____

Have you had someone from your past that wasn't a love interest become a love interest later down the line? How did it work out?

_____

_____

_____

www.thecmwexperience.com

Check out the blog section of the book's website for the full experience.

Why Run

YOU WANT TO play hard to get?
    Okay, I get it!
    What I don't get is, why.
Why do you proceed with this game?
. . . This chase?
With hopes that I will persist and proceed to pursue,
With blisters on my feet from this hunt,
You return simply to show me that I'm close,
To show me you want me.
Like a treat dangling in front of a fat kid on a treadmill.
But in this case, it wasn't for this fat kid's greater good.
. . . Fat from the false-hope fries, the same-old-game shakes,
The BS burgers, and the usual almost-there apple pies.
But now, I've lost weight along with patience and time.
I've outrun the treadmill, and now my pride is catching up.

What I don't get about this chase is why I keep running
Knowing you and what you will do.
Is it that I see something in you that could fit the future?
Could it be that I stopped chasing cars and started chasing a house . . .
A long-term investment?
Or is it just that?
Is it the chase that leads to a prize worth pursuing?

I got it . . .

It's a lot simpler.

I caught a whiff of something that began to tickle all my senses

The more I explored.

So why deprive my instincts?

Maybe you're expecting an answer.

Maybe you're expecting me to end with a positive note or a compliment.

Smiles . . . well, no.

Because that would only be more energy spent chasing you,

And I'm done running.

My feet are already moving in a new direction.

I guess it's "tag, you're it . . ."

What's Up? Talk to Me! Why Run

We've sort of discussed this already, but let's continue to be honest and transparent here. The male is, and historically has been, the pursuer, 98.989 percent (embellished stat) of the time. However, it may not always be the case. So I'll separate the questions by *pursuer* and *pursued*. Regardless of which you are, you can give the answer you think the other party would provide.

Pursuer: If someone continues to lead you on a chase, but never complies, when do you decide to end your chase? What signs do you look for, especially when they claim they are into you?

Pursued: At what point does playing hard to get stop for you? What were your reasons for doing so in the first place: the benefits, the attention, it was fun, didn't know how to say no, didn't want to be mean, didn't realize it, etc.?

---

www.thecmwexperience.com

Check out the blog section of the book's website for the full experience.

Guilty

GUILTY, FOR ACTIONS I didn't commit.
Judged by a jury of my peers.
Typo—judged by a jury of *your friends*.
With no witnesses and no victims to speak of
. . . How?
How was I branded with the title of the "bad guy"?
The burning metal singes my flesh.
The tearing away of more flesh as time passes, but
The pain becomes more bearable as I see a chance to clear my name.
I take the stand.
At first, my words fall upon deaf ears.
Then like water into pores, it sinks in.
Washing away the negativity makeup your friends put on your face.
Yet the past whispers in your ear, "Guilty."
However, my past has a voice too, and he whispers simultaneously, "Guilty."
I'm guilty of (K)aring (A)bout (Y)ou (L)ately (A)bove all.
I'm guilty by association.
Maybe I'm guilty of identity fraud.
Wait! I know I'm not him.
You may still be in the Halloween spirit, but
I'm not going to wear a mask of someone I'm not.
It's okay though.
I'm a billionaire in the making, so I can pay the bail.
I won't be jail mate 909 (only you would get that).

What's Up? Talk to Me! Guilty

Have you been in a situation where someone you're dealing with formed a false opinion of you? Also that opinion was based solely upon an associate you both mutually knew. Tell me your story. They may have jumped to conclusions, but I'll hear you out.

To make my case worse, the woman I was dealing with, along with her friends, had an "all men are dogs" mentality.

---

www.thecmwexperience.com

Check out the blog section of the book's website for the full experience.

Timing

*T*ICK, GRR . . . *tock, grrr . . . tick, grrrr . . . tock, grrrrr.*
A consistent slow and salient sound grows with every second.
An arm that never rests,
No matter how much you crave a chance to catch your breath.
Tick.
It rotates with no signs of remorse or compassion.
Free and without limitation, the tick knows no meaning of the words
Stop, pause, or *freeze.*
Tick.
With every small motion, you lose another small piece of time, yet
You gain more time with pain and more time without her.
It lies dormant in the pit of your stomach.
Tick!
Do you poke a sleeping bear while it is hibernating?
But with no use for words like *fear*, the arm follows every tick
With a poke and every tock with a jab at this beastly bear.
Tock!
The ticks grow louder. The tocks grow louder. The pain grows angrier.
None of them care about who is at fault . . . none care about why or how.
Tick.
How did the two meet anyway? Time should not know pain!
Did he forget his occupation? Time is supposed to heal all wounds.
Was it that it was bad timing?

Is this how Time spends his days off —antagonizing (still ticking)?

Tick.

The beast known as pain?

Wrong timing?

Could timing be the reason this situation was even given life?

Was it not the right time for her or . . . for me?

Bad timing for us?

Grrr . . .but no time for regrets, the clock's arm

Has no need for such things!

Maybe with Time as our counselor, we could find time

For a future together.

The ticks won't stop, but maybe they don't need to!

Tick.

. . . Because at some point, Time returns to work and begins healing.

. . . Someone has to cater to this beast.

. . . God is the only one who can manipulate time.

His plan has both of our best interests at heart.

So I place my trust in His timing.

Tock.

What's Up? Talk to Me! Timing

Have you ever felt like you met the right person at the wrong time?

_____

Tell me about it.

_____

Why was it the wrong time?

_____

What could have made it the right time?

_____

What made them the right person?

_____

_____

_____

www.thecmwexperience.com

Check out the blog section of the book's website for the full experience.

The Waiter and the Difficult Customer

HOW DOES IT feel to be his waiter?

Indecisive and indeterminate

Seems to describe this customer all too well.

Hungry and thirsty

With a desire to excite his taste buds—that's easy to tell

. . . but not easy to cater.

He desires a taste to remember and savor!

He has the power to control minds.

He's a courageous, confident, conquering, caring,

Compassionate, confused, core, and headache.

And he can't seem to be fully satisfied with the menu.

Which are the reasons he continues:

To get you in trouble

To compare his meal to others

To remember failed entrées

To allow his curiosity to double.

Well, they say the customer is always right!

In fact, maybe the issue is the restaurant of Life

That he has been attending for the last twenty-two years.

You've worked tirelessly out of the same restaurant for twenty-two years

Just trying to do right,

Trying to do right by your first and most influential customer.

He has now encompassed experiences with expectations and

Even evidence in the last few nights.

Consequently, he has discovered some sort of discernment and

Formulated some sort of preference or idea of what he has a taste for.

You say, "Sure."

Then, you look in the restaurant of Life,

Checking in the back for what's in store.

You bring him a few entrée:

He prays with them . . . (typo) for them . . . (typo) over them.

He appreciates their flavor and even adds to their recipe.

Yet, he calls you.

He signals you closer and says, "Don't have a cow,

But, I simply wasn't wowed."

Still not quite pleased yet,

This customer that most refer to as the **Heart**, his only tip,

To keep looking.

What's Up? Talk to Me! The Waiter and the Difficult Customer

I feel as though we all go through this period, maybe multiple times in our lives. Have you ever felt you knew or had an idea of what you were looking for in a companion, yet your heart just never seemed to be satisfied?

_____

Tell me about those moments.

_____

_____

_____

www.thecmwexperience.com

Check out the blog section of the book's website for the full experience.

What His Silence Says

WORDS AREN'T EXCHANGED.
    At least not externally, because currently, that currency
    Is being exchanged in his head.
A luxury he unfortunately can't afford for her.
Wait, what was just said? A luxury or a tragedy.
He is overwhelmed drowning in his own thoughts of her,
As she sits there
Every thought of a word that begins to form becomes a blur,
As new thoughts flow in.
They are all joyful thoughts, but what's the cause of the silence?
Could it be that her beauty has taken his wind?
Or is it as simple as her mere presence taking a toll?
He spends time with his heart racing, but even with all this drive,
He still loses control.
Her smile is so cultivating that when it emerges, it begins orchestrating
A symphony of love songs.
Has he been sitting in silence for too long?
It's in this moment he chooses to bask.
Now he toggles back and forth between the pros and cons
Like a game of Ping-Pong
To avoid being fooled by a mask.
Then he's appalled by this thought
Because with flaws and all, time with her is still like a resort.

It's a getaway.

It's fun.

It's a giveaway

That you've won.

It's the perfect day,

And she's the sun.

What's unfortunate is, these are all things she doesn't know . . .

"Hello."

"Are you okay?"

The words formulate

As if the following words were fate.

You say,

"Yeah, I'm *great*."

But words from you would not be something she needed to seek,

If only your silence

Could speak.

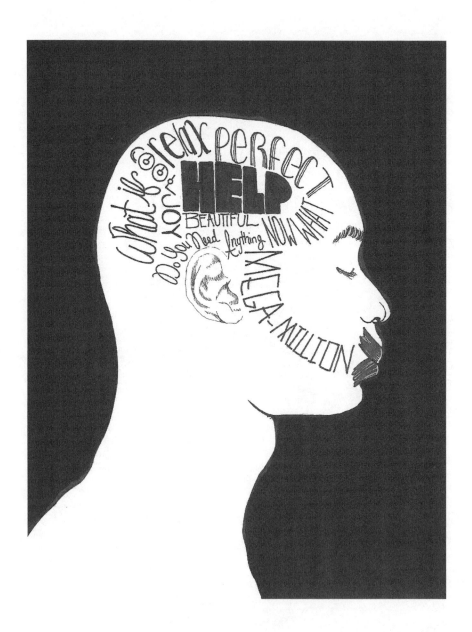

What's Up? Talk to Me!   What His Silence Says

Have you ever been with someone and you could not read their silence? Ladies, if he's really into you and just enjoying the moment, his silence could just be a positive outline of his thoughts of you.

_____

What else do you think he is thinking?

_____

Fellas, have you ever been speechless or spoke less than normal when with someone you really liked? Tell me about it.

_____

_____

_____

www.thecmwexperience.com

Check out the blog section of the book's website for the full experience.

2:23 a.m.

I TRY TO FIND the words to say.
How'd I even give this much of my heart away?
Or maybe it was taken.
Or maybe it's the time and effort you put in that had me thinking.
Maybe it was the heart of gold that radiated from your chest.
It illuminates at its highest frequency when your hand
And head is pressed against my chest.
Frequently fathoming a future,
While you are still stagnantly stepping through the past.
With only our present left to suffer the blow.
If a roadblock is what you see, but a doorway is what I choose to be,
Then going ghost is what I will achieve.
But before I disappear into thin air,
Let me break it down like a compactor.
First, you must have worked like a contractor
The way you put in more work than Rihanna.
Not quite as much as I, yet your effort never lost my eye.
Could it be your voice that emits pure forms of love,
Or the soul-gripping hugs?
Our hugs fit and form to our bodies like a glove.
Which only makes catching you in my arms that much better.
It's possible I've struck myself out and you're in need of a new batter.
Is this because I wasn't able to remove your fear of getting hurt?

Because I couldn't remove the fear that things could change?

Or because by cuffing me, your academic life would have been chained?

Growth is all I've ever promoted, but it is now what I seem to hinder.

Your gifts are what I tried to help you find,

But we're always so far from December.

Soon you will be great.

The date is unknown, but I cannot wait.

I try to create a mirror, so you can see what I see

. . . Past your hurt and pain.

I'm not quite sure what I want, which is part of the blame.

Maybe this is not what I want,

But there was always something special about you that I did.

Yet be that as it may . . .

I can only push you up, never away,

Because your glow is a light I want to stay.

Maybe it's that spark I'm looking for that keeps us at bay.

Now our light is what seems to fade away.

2:23 a.m. Just my thoughts.

What's Up? Talk to Me! 2:23 a.m.

Has the night ever caused an idle mind to drift in a sea of thoughts and ideas that wash on the shore of the person in your life at the time causing all thoughts to be centered around them?

_____

What were you thinking?

_____

Did anything trigger it?

_____

_____

_____

www.thecmwexperience.com

Check out the blog section of the book's website for the full experience.

In Love or Just Inspired

D O YOU REMEMBER your first time being in love?

That overwhelming feeling of joy you were submerged into when you were around that special person?

It was as if their presence had a radiating wavelength that sent a signal to your brain that said, "smile, now laugh" every time.

Then without a second thought, impulses were sent from your brain to your mouth and, finally, to your heart.

You don't know the feeling. It's new to your mind, but somewhat familiar to your heart,

As if you had experienced something relatively close to it.

Waking up to thoughts of them in the morning.

Gripping your pillow so tight you could feel your favorite features of their body in your arms.

Like a fly to a windshield, thoughts of what they are doing collided with your peace of mind during the nighttime.

When finding them on your timeline was so exciting, your friends would have thought their post went viral.

However, the feeling didn't start this strong. So you wouldn't share how you feel with many others, especially not with that special person.

At least, not until you were sure of who this stranger was in your heart, occupying more and more space.

It was a seed that was planted after that first moment of fun, laughter, and maybe more.

It's watered by the small things and nourished by the big things that special person did.

So, when was this happening?

It happened as time passed that they would:

Take the time to learn your favorite snack, candy, or meal,

Take the initiative to learn specific body gestures so they would know when you were down, sad, excited, nervous, or uncomfortable.

They would believe you could when even you were unsure if you could.

The crazy thing was, simultaneously, you found yourself doing these exact same things . . . maybe even before they started.

When time spent with them felt like time spent with one of your closest friends and yet time with someone who was so much more.

Do you remember this feeling?

I don't . . .

I've never been in love.

. . . Well, I had a taste of something close. How else could I know some of these moments and feelings?

The "situationship" came with your standard installments of rough patches, and ups and downs.

She was an amazing girl, but . . .

Trust and insecurities were molehills that became mountains.

One of those feelings I was unable to strengthen; the other I was unable to weaken.

I was guilty of that, but my intentions were always those of joy, not pain. At times, I would make it worse.

The biggest issue was not these two factors. It was that there was something missing.

The thing that was missing was probably the cause of those two factors.

What was I missing?

Do you remember the cartoons or movies where there were huge piles of TNT, dynamite, or gasoline?

A monumental, exciting, action-packed, illuminated explosion with the potential of changing everything within its blast radius was waiting.

But what was missing?

What was missing was a feeling of certainty that said, "This is where I know I want to be."

A feeling that said, "This is the one, *finally*." "This was meant for me."

Above all, it would say, "Now I'm done searching."

What those cartoon explosions were missing was a spark, and so was I. What I remember is, she was the first (at the moment, the only) one to bring me that close to being in love.

Loving someone and being in love are different. I guess I was just inspired . . .

What's Up? Talk to Me!   In Love or Just Inspired

Do feel like you know what love is and how it should feel?

_____

Have you ever been in love?

_____

How do you know?

_____

How can you be sure of this?

_____

_____

_____

www.thecmwexperience.com

Check out the blog section of the book's website for the full experience.

February 14

WHETHER IT IS a conundrum causing confusion
Or feelings of forging your own freedom
That has caused us division and you to be alone on this day,
Those feelings are now trumped by this day of affection.
As if without casting a vote,
This new notion stole the election.
It now governs your views on this special 14th day.

It also affects my views.
You deserve to feel desired
On this day of compassion, devotion, love, and affection.
With a big head and an even bigger heart,
You stand beautifully made
And perfectly designed.

And I just wanted to convey these sentiments from **A** to **E**, whether
Or not you're mine:
An admiration administered for how you **apply** yourself . . .
It **behooves** me to **bask** in your **bountiful blessings.**
Carefully concentrating on eternal beauty that **constitutes** your **charisma**
While **directing** all **doubtful, distracting, divided** thoughts **downward.**
Every piece of **evidence** used to **evaluate** your **excellence** makes it **evident**
That you deserve to feel special on this special day.
Happy Valentine's Day!

What's Up? Talk to Me!   February 14

It may not be your day, but that doesn't mean it's not your season!

Do you consider Valentine's Day to be a powerful day of compassion, devotion, love, and affection? Why or Why not?

Tell me about your best February 14 – V-Day.

Tell me about your worst February 14 – V-Day.

---

www.thecmwexperience.com

Check out the blog section of the book's website for the full experience.

Save the Hero

YOU DO . . . . You do again!
You do some more . . . . And that's all you do.
You give, then you keep on giving.
Now you're by no means perfect . . . but what hero is?
You uncover their biggest fears,
So that you can use your super strength to protect them.
You discover their favorite colors,
So that you can warp reality and make those colors appear everywhere.
You decipher their body language,
So now as the greatest detective the world has ever seen,
You can tell when they are happy, sad, upset, or just playing games.
You use your super speed to make sure they have their favorite
Flowers or candy when they least expect it.
Your powers know no bounds and are no stranger to versatility.
Why?
Because your abilities don't stop there.
With your invulnerability, you withstand every shot or blow they throw
In your direction, and you're still able and willing to be there for them.
Maybe the credit for that belongs to your healing factor.
You can hide any pain or weakness behind your invisibility.
You have the ability to see their true heart using X-ray vision.
However, your greatest ability is your compassion for them
And all they believe in.

But what happens when you take off

Your costume – when you take off your super suit?

What happens when your healing factor wears off

And your strength fades?

When wounds from your circumstances won't heal?

When pushing through becomes like pushing a mountain?

What happens when your invisibility wears off, but

No one can decipher *your* signals for help?

When the smile you hide behind becomes smaller?

When you want to share what it is that you're bothered about,

But pride won't let you, or

You don't know how, and maybe

You don't see why?

When you won't give in to self-pity,

And you don't want to be a burden?

Who saves the hero?

What's Up? Talk to Me!   Save the Hero

Can you relate to being the one to invest the most and provide the most effort in a relationship? For example, conversations are completely centered around the other party, as are outings and gift giving. In return, the bare minimum is given, just enough to show mutual interest or some interest. Yet, the farther you go down this road, the more you see signs that say it is still just a one-way road.

Share your experiences.

Did they ever reciprocate the same effort?

Would you let these moments stop you from investing in others in the future? Could this stop you from investing in the right ones in the future?

Tell me why.

Have you ever been the one receiving without putting forth the effort? Tell me the story?

Did you start putting forth effort? If so, what caused the change?

www.thecmwexperience.com

Check out the blog section of the book's website for the full experience.

Pity Party

CATACLYSMIC!
It's a catastrophe!
"Woe is me!"
Or is it just some BS?
Thoughts formulated in my head,
But they also seep in from my chest.
Home alone,
But alone I'm not.
I'm accompanied by many thoughts.
All in one central spot,
They stream in and crash.

Exterior, calm.
Motion, idle.
Nothing rash.
Internally, much more lively,
Like the family known as the brass.
Sometimes more like the strings,
But here's the thing,
Despite all the music
It's not all bad.
Things are just amplified by the music outside your head.

Your likely location is in bed,

Or someplace comfortable

Surrounded by the sounds of

Smooth songs,

Slow songs,

Sappy songs,

Love songs.

Your thoughts react like a bad chemistry experiment.

Now what you don't have,

And what you want

Create your new sentiments.

They meet and they compare

Thoughts no one else can hear.

That means to soliloquize.

You're talking to yourself.

Now the feeling of what you want begins to tantalize,

Or is it another star too far out of reach,

As the songs continue to preach.

Think, is there really such a thing as out of reach,

But only you can answer that for yourself.

Just think about it . . .

Then think about the limitations

You placed on your wings.

What's Up? Talk to Me! Pity Party

If we aren't cool by now, one of us is not fully invested in the conversation. I'm just saying! Here is more about me. I despise throwing myself pity parties. I try to practice what I preach—find the bright side, try not to take things personal, be open to different perspectives and possibilities, and most importantly, I try to laugh. At times, even I feel the need to partake in some of the festivities, but I always keep it short.

How do you crash, end, or leave your own pity party, or do you just stay until it's over?

---

www.thecmwexperience.com

Check out the blog section of the book's website for the full experience.

Aware of the Feels

I FEEL NOTHING.
I am filled with nothing.
I have no room for weakness.
The sign hung across my chest says,
"We have the right to refuse service to anyone."
So, I refuse to feed into feelings.
Do you get it?

By allowing feelings to seep in
Deeper and deeper
Like a knife,
The more painful its removal
Will feel.

The more you fill yourself with them,
The emptier you'll feel when their dispensed.
So, I won't fill, so I don't feel.

A stone knows no weakness, only
Strength.
Dense, stable, and unaffected by what happens to or around it.
A flower knows no strength, only
Vulnerability and weakness.

Affected by what happens to and around it.

What's the difference?

Weakness

And not being weak.

But which of the two is actually stronger

. . . Because only one of the two can become something more by blossoming.

I will not relinquish power or control.

I will not give in to feelings.

This is my life,

My body,

My store,

And we refuse such customers.

Read the sign!

This is the "man's burden,"

Right?

That's my role – a role I have no problem playing.

A role that was contaminated.

Unaware of the fact that I have succumbed to its venom.

Unaware of the fact that I have written this under its influence.

And unaware of the pros

While being conned by the cons.

But

Aware that I do feel,

And

Aware that I don't want to . . .

Now you get it.

Contrary to how it may seem from some of these stories, I (probably like most men) don't enjoy giving in to my emotions. I'm not referring to the positive or joyful ones. I'm referring to the ones associated with being vulnerable. The ones that reveal there is something wrong; the emotions associated with sensitivity. When I do drown in emotions, I use altered perspectives, faith, and some positive triggers to stay afloat and find land. However, you are never allowed to see that outside of this book. It's as if my mantra is "never let them see you sweat." I have a double standard for myself when it comes to these emotions. To me, it's perfectly fine for anyone else to display emotions, regardless of the why, how, gender, race, age, religion. However, it's not okay for me to feed into the emotions or show them when I do. I'm still a work in progress. (WIP).

I wanted to share more about myself since you've been sharing (hopefully) so much up to this point.

_____

What's your take on what I've shared?

_____

_____

_____

www.thecmwexperience.com

Check out the blog section of the book's website for the full experience.

There's No Coal in Your Stocking

WHAT IF I told you love wasn't real?

What if I told you love was like Santa Claus?

We were raised and conditioned to believe in Santa

At a young age.

Vast physical representations of a force and

A person that no one has seen,

Events held in his honor,

And gatherings and gifts because of his mere essence.

For many, with age comes doubt of his existence.

With age, comes the desire for proof.

You're surrounded by these people who blindly believe and those who

Have lost all faith.

Who do you listen to?

Eventually, your parents tell you he's not real.

If not them, then it's your friends or society who tell you so.

But what of love?

Who tells you whether or not it exists if you haven't discovered it yet?

Who do you listen to?

They never say, "it's not real."

What if I told you love was real?

What if I told you love was like Santa Claus?

Can you recall the Christmas movies

Where Santa's strength was derived from everyone's belief in him?

Believe in love! Give love!

I don't know how or when, but it's coming.

Be willing to receive love.

Embrace love!

And at some point . . . you'll see some proof in your stocking.

What's Up? Talk to Me!   There's No Coal in Your Stocking

Here I want to encourage those in search of love.

I'm in a "go with the flow" stage, but I must ask, "do you think love is something to believe in?" Of course, I would need you to tell me your reasons why.

---

www.thecmwexperience.com

Check out the blog section of the book's website for the full experience.

Just Thought You Should Know

TO BE HONEST, you are really pissing me off, and I hope you read this! I am extremely curious about what you have been doing all this time. But allow me to reveal to you what I have been doing this entire time. Waiting . . .

Yet I haven't been waiting patiently because I've also been looking.

The issue is, I can't get over the fact that

Your mere presence could bring me joy.

You could actually be my lady and my friend.

Wait, "and my friend?"

Do you understand that you are fulfilling two vital roles in my life?

That means I can always be myself around you.

I know you may be expecting big words or deep metaphors, but

It's simpler than that.

You are what makes me happy and whole.

The gear that keeps my watch running!

So without you, time stops . . .

This may seem a little dramatic to some,

But this is not meant for them . . .

It's meant for you.

The "yes, you can" in my ear . . . no, the "yes, you will" in my ear.

The teeth in my smile.

The sound in my laugh.

In other words, the things that are needed for simple expressions of joy.

I still added metaphors anyway, I know.

Just know the person I want to spend most of my time with is you.

Except when it's guy time, of course,

But even then, I'd talk about you.

And when its grind time,

But even there, you'd be a factor in my motivation.

Or when it's me time,

But even then, you would still be on my mind.

So I guess that means my original statement still stands -

"The person I want to spend most of my time with is you."

You, the understanding, (relatively) open-minded, fun comedian.

At least, you'll probably think you're funny.

You, the beauty and the brains.

. . . You.

If we don't cross paths, don't worry about me.

I'll make the most of a bachelor's life, believe you me.

I'll still achieve greatness and happiness.

The difference with and without you, respectively,

Is like chasing your dreams and being part of the nation's top 5% or

Chasing your dreams and starting from the bottom up.

The difference is the advantage.

To be clear and not to scare,

I'm not speaking of marriage. I'm talking about a connection,

A feeling that says, "this is who you should be with right now,

Without a doubt . . ."

So!

We may or may not have met.
We may already know each other well or not at all.
I don't know who, what, when, or how . . .
What I know is that you're mine. So well . . .
Stop playing games, lady! We have history to make!

What's Up? Talk to Me!   Just Thought You Should Know

During your single moments, did you or have you wondered what your future lady or man was doing with their life prior to your meeting?

_____

What were some of the things that crossed your mind?

_____

_____

_____

www.thecmwexperience.com

Check out the blog section of the book's website for the full experience.

For You: The Untold Story

PRESSURE ON COAL creates diamonds.

So what has you stressed?

Life taking its shots at you?

My arms will cover you as a bulletproof vest.

So with every test,

With every obstacle,

When all life's rain becomes the forest that is tropical,

I'll clear the pain from the rain off your face like a topical.

I'll lead you out of this forest

And not walk but run to the Lord,

While living a life that rejects the idea of being bored.

Let me motivate that motor

And fuel that fire.

Let me encourage your drive,

So that your engine keeps running, and you never feel empty.

But you still don't get me.

You need to know that, with me, you're stripped of the option

To settle.

So no more bronze or silver,

Only gold metals.

You know what, scratch that. The point I am trying to make here is simple. I'm here for you because you were made for me. I'm your Adam, and you're my Eve. Do you remember that story of how God took Adam's rib in order to bless him with his Eve? Well, here's what you weren't aware of:

When Eve was tempted by the snake, which was really the gecko from the GEICO commercial (I know, crazy, right?), I know Adam knew something was wrong. You may be wondering how. Was it an instinctive gut feeling? No. The events that transpired that we weren't informed of was that the same gecko (yes, the one from the commercial) actually tried to persuade Adam initially. However, there was no way to sway or woo Adam because he realized the severity of the situation. The person who told Adam not to was God, and the person trying to convince him otherwise was a gecko, who only saved him "15 percent or more" on clothes at the time, but Adam and Eve didn't even know what the word *naked* meant before being introduced to the fruit. Consequently, the gecko had no choice but to use his nefarious, razor-sharp tongue on Eve. The crazy thing about that situation is Eve's discipline and gut instincts would have prevailed if it wasn't for the one thing the gecko promised the apple could do. Among the vast number of so-called abilities that the fruit possessed, the false one that the gecko promised was the knowledge of how to prevent God from creating another woman with another one of Adam's ribs (c'mon, really, Eve?). As a result, she bit into the fruit. In addition, the gecko conveniently forgot to mention to Eve that Adam also had to bite into the confines of the fruit. Once he disclosed this to Eve, she was off to convince Adam. Eve relayed the entire story of the fruit and gecko to Adam (minus the "other woman prevention" part, of course). Adam knew in his mind not to trust this devious creature, but it was his heart that was running the show. Eve offered Adam a bite. Completely submerged in his love for Eve while drowning in her eyes, his thoughts of the consequences of his actions became more convoluted than mixing hot sauce and baby oil in your cereal. Adam completely forgot that he was instructed not to, as did Eve. Adam replied with his hand extended and his eyes still locked to hers, "For you, anything"— with his intentions being purely to convey feelings of support, trust, confidence (in her), open-mindedness, and love.

I'm sure by now you may have guessed that isn't exactly how the original story went, and the gecko is not really evil (he actually seems really cool). Now, I am in no way saying we will be disobeying God. I merely wanted to paint a picture to show your value in my eyes. I was simply trying to emphasize that for you—anything.

What's Up? Talk to Me!   For You: The Untold Story

Here I want to let her know (whoever she is) that she's joining the winning team and what she is getting herself into.

_____

If there was a pamphlet that summarized what being with you would be like, what would it say? What would be in it?

_____

_____

_____

www.thecmwexperience.com

Check out the blog section of the book's website for the full experience.

Graduate Cheat Sheet

THE ANSWER IS yes! "Yes?"

Yes.

Yes, there is heartbreak and heartache.

Yes, there is heart warmth.

Yes, there are feelings of bliss.

Yes, there are feelings of sadness.

Yes, there are feelings of discouragement and doubt.

Yes, there are feelings of confidence and certainty.

Yes, there is compromise.

Yes, there are concrete decisions.

Yes, acceptance exists.

Yes, rejection exists.

Yes, simplicity exists.

Yes, complication exists.

Yes, you can be single as long as you want.

Yes, you can desire a relationship.

Yes, others may not see what you see in a person.

Yes, others may see what you can't see in a person.

Yes, friends and family may despise them.

Yes, friends and family may love them.

Yes, this list is long.

No, this is not everything.

The point is, there are good and bad, pros and cons.

Just make the most of the journey and the people in it.

The destination has no value without the journey.

Nor can it be reached without a journey.

So . . .

Live *your* life and learn to appreciate

The unpredictable voyage, flight, tour, expedition, passage, ride, drive –

The journey

Once again, let me just be the first to say, you did it! Just to share a little more about my journey—this journey had a lot of great people and moments that weren't shared! The moments conveyed here are those that I wrote when I was strongly inspired. For me, sometimes hard times are the easiest stories to tell. Plus, pain sounds better on paper.

Any other topics you want me to cover?

_____

_____

_____

www.thecmwexperience.com

Check out the blog section of the book's website for the full experience.

Turn the page.

The end . . . hold on, wait!

Before You Go – My Self-Evaluation

S IMILAR TO THE classroom, in life we are all met with tests and evaluations. I'm assuming what I had encountered and am about to share was my final exam. The difficulty level was like that of a graduate course for a freshman. However, I could never even fathom the idea of a "pop final" (pop quiz and final exam combined). I say that because I was blindsided like a deer who thought it was safe to cross the road. Yet, I was not ill-prepared. So, before you go, witness my self-evaluation where a particular turn of events caused pain/anger to test me on all that I have learned from my journey of growth and love.

A master's in love, you say? There seemed to be a positive ending to these messages, entertaining encounters for the masses, and heart-felt tear jerkers for whoever your future special lady will be. However, have we missed something? What a turn of events. You better grab the steering wheel and brace for impact. Your last few pieces gave notes to Miss Right, but Miss Right "now" left you almost empty-handed. With what warmth do you have left to give? What use is a cold shoulder to cry on? You can't end it. Explain this to the people . . . don't worry, they read this far. We'll all wait. Let's talk about the only woman you've let get this close to your heart. Tell them what just happened, or should I? You can't even find a solid emotion to invest in, but you can bank on one thing . . . she's happy. How could she not be, she was with him! He has a condo in the city with the wealthy, and the standard luxury corporate company car. Wait, tell me again what year and model was his new BMW? Maybe it's because he's an engineer. I guess her new man beat you there . . . by like 14 years. You preached about growth, then let's look on the bright side—at least you knew this was going on. Oh, no you didn't. Oh wait, she was still messing with you during this time. Sorry, I'm mixing up sob stories. Well, you guys never were officially together, right? Sounds like a "situationship" that turned into a situation. Oh no, wait! You guys were exclusive, which was her idea right? Wasn't she the first girl you've loved or the first that "inspired love" according to you? The circumstances are irrelevant—all that how long, how close, "I would never," and agreements, blah, blah, blah, etc.

They're only important to you, not the situation. Well, and maybe to anyone else in the same

predicament. That's beside the point. Should I share more about him? Maybe we should talk sheets and covers?

When I would weight train, my coach always said, "Pain is just weakness leaving the body." Consequently, it takes strength, will, and desire to overcome anything from a misplaced heart to a traumatic life-and-death experience. It takes strength not to change who you are as a person. That same strength is needed to change into the person you and all the people around you always knew you would be: strength to stay steadfast on your goals; strength to see it from her point of view; and strength to be happy for her.

Ha ha, you're right about everything, except you're missing a few details. Here is where you're wrong. An engineer? He did not beat me there. An engineer is a single category that would not do my greatness any justice. I am an engineer, an entrepreneur, a creator, a philanthropist, a motivational speaker, an investor, a prayer intercessor, an app inventor, a video game creator, a clothing-line designer, a scriptwriter, a CEO, and a published author to say the least. A bachelor's and a master's do not mean I have all the answers in life and love. Similar to how a few years at an institution does not constitute a student becoming a perfect employee or CEO. It simply means I've fundamentally gone through the proper channels of education—life. I've learned to embrace the journey. I've learned how to see into the future. How do you do that? By creating it!

What's Up? Talk to Me!   Before You Go

Boom! You thought we were done? Well, we are now.

The strength in my final assessment could be misleading. I did not completely skip the grieving process. This was the heaviest of any of the other situations and stories. One reason was because the emotional depth of the situation was new. She made it past more barriers and walls than anyone else had ever done. Consequently, she was the only person that appeared more than once in this book. It wasn't an immediate pain, as the adrenaline of the moment repelled the negative thoughts and questions—that is, until reality set in. Like healed broken bones in cold weather, it ached and pained even after I thought it had fully healed. Small things became triggers that reminded me of what had happened. Yet I did heal, and the incident has become a distant memory. So I regret nothing. This situation happened as I was concluding this journey. It was the final accumulative exam and the perfect ending.

I don't think bad decisions always make a bad person. What do you think?

---

www.thecmwexperience.com

Check out the blog section of the book's website for the full experience.

Congrats! You've been awarded your Master's in Love.

The University of Life

THE FACULTY OF THE UNIVERSITY OF LIFE
HEREBY ADMIT

_____

TO THE DEGREE OF

Love Degree

Master of Romance in Love

God

Carl M. Watson

_____
President Of The University of Life

_____
Dean Of The College

These three people are my three pillars:

Grandma (Love): "I'll always love you."

Mom (Faith): "Even in this, God is."

Dad (Confidence): "Small things to a giant."

I would like to acknowledge, thank, and praise two very special artist. The two that took my vision for the book cover and artwork and gave them life:

Lianne Smith (@dashofartistry) - The brilliance behind the artistry within the book.

Cornell McGowan - The genius behind the book's front cover.

I want to also give a special thanks and acknowledgment to you reading this. A special thanks for finishing the book, and a special acknowledgment for finishing strong in your own obstacles and struggles up to this point in your life. Aye, great job and thank you!